DEAR S
A MANUAL FOR THE
RIGHTFUL ART OF DYING

Translator's Note

Finality in translation must remain unattainable. Behind Martin Moller's style, literary diction, and usage lies a sense of timelessness and universality which only compounds the challenges of translation. My continued search for more distinct and tangible equivalencies has led me to the overwhelming and often disabling sense of our languages' ever-present flux, whether in print on the pages of the outgoing sixteenth century or in the process of writing presently at the outset of the third millennium.

I value learning from critical readers.

Selfishly, I hope for their responses to be gentle.

Many, many thanks to the meaningful encouragements I received during this project's journey. I thank Suzanne George for her firm faith in my efforts. I also thank Sheila Perryman for her tireless work in making my semantic meanderings more approachable to contemporary readers. To my sisters Katrine and Ruth, and to my brothers Daniel and David, a wholehearted *thank you* for your unyielding support. Most principally, I *thank you* – Kim, Kate, Neil, and Sam – your brave patience is truly humbling.

Finally, a word of admiration for the typesetters of the early generation printing presses as they composed movable type by hand into cast metal sorts and thereby molded words and lines of reversed text into what would turn out to be astonishingly lucid pages. Their labor I regard as nothing less than heroic. Their skill –usually altogether unacknowledged– has permitted the privilege of timelessness.

Stephen Trobisch

DEAR SOUL

A Manual for the Rightful Art of Dying

Martin Moller

Compiled by Suzanne George
Translated by Stephen Trobisch
Edited by Sheila Perryman
Introduced by Austra Reinis

Quiet Waters Publications
Bolivar, Missouri
2014

Quiet Waters Publications
P.O. Box 34, Bolivar, MO 65613-0034

www.quietwaterspub.com

Cover Design:
> Cynthia Johnson
> Jay Nicholson
> Jeff Williams
> Daniel Wedlock
> Suzanne George

Translated from the original German by
> Stephen Trobisch

Edited by
> Sheila Perryman

Introduction by
> Austra Reinis

ISBN 978-1-931475-65-5
Library of Congress Control Number: 2014911754

Dedication

I dedicate this book to my Mom Sandra, my children, Manda,
Daniel and Derick, my son-in-law Daniel, my grandchildren,
my brother Danny, and my late father Floyd. In recognition
of the beloved Martin Moller and of all the loved ones
who are no longer with us.
Suzanne George

To the only wise God our Savior, be glory and majesty, domin-
ion and power, both now and ever.

Amen, Amen, Amen!

A Journey of Nearly 500 Years

Prologue
by Suzanne George

I am that *simple-minded lay person*. I am that person for whom Martin Moller wrote this book. With the Lord Jesus Christ as my savior, I pray for eternal life. This book has provided me with great comfort and peace. I knew that it was my task to make the *Manuale* available to English readers and that it had to be completed.

I have spent more than 20 years in the presence of this volume, consisting of three books, without fully comprehending its contents. Through grace and wisdom I have learned that *not* knowing everything is alright – and it takes courage to say that. Faith and a teachable heart provide everything needed for growth. In my own way with my heart, my mind, and my faith I kept translating the book's content; nevertheless, I had to know more. Five years ago, this volume was handed to me with love and devotion. "It is your time," Mom said, "the *Manuale* is the inspired word of GOD through Martin Moller." My task became daunting. Not completing it, however, was my *only* fear.

Translating the German text into English became my calling and charge. I contacted the Library of Congress, seminaries, and universities all over the country to seek out help. Although unable to offer much practical assistance –based on the volume's age and scarcity of references– these institutions offered encouragement. I then contacted organizations outside of the United States, but even The Gutenberg Museum graciously pointed out that only little information is available; the cover page of the volume's 3rd book, the *Manuale*, has no indication of a date. Eventually, we located an electronic scan of the *Manuale's* initial publication as a single book at the Bayrische Staatsbibliothek in Munich. It dates back to 1593.

Finally, under God's guidance, I contacted Missouri State University in Springfield and at long last – a breakthrough! Dr. Stephen Trobisch was highly recommended by the Modern and Classical Languages Department. We met in 2011, and the project moved into a pivotal beginning. We hired Sheila Perryman, editor and research assistant, in 2012. The *Manuale* has taken almost four years to prepare for publication. Both, the *Manuale* (the volume's 3rd part) and the *Holy Contemplation* (2nd part) are translated into English. Completing the *Evangelium* (1st part) may take several years. I cannot put into words my appreciation for the painstaking diligence our team has devoted to the project. All the hours, weeks, and months of the past two years' benevolent labor and preparation seem difficult to comprehend; and how astonishing that *all members* of our team live in the State of Missouri! This endeavor, I hope, will remain a lifelong project for all.

The volume handed down to me has the three works by Martin Moller slightly bound and threaded together. The *Evangelium* alone has 1,115 pages, and it contains impressive visual artwork for each Gospel passage applied in individual sermons. The *Holy Contemplation* contains accounts and exegeses of events before, during, and after Christ's crucifixion. The *Manuale* –the 3rd book you are now reading– offers a *salutary* preparation for the stages of death and dying in nine chapters.

Great care was given to reproduce the artwork and to adapt the formatting of the text from the original to a more modern layout. We meticulously researched and footnoted all scriptural references to help readers of the *Manuale* peruse the context of the quoted Bible passages simultaneously. We decided to add verse numbers to Martin Moller's chapter references as an aid to modern readers. We attempted to preserve Martin Moller's textual presentation as authentically as possible, including punctuation marks and variable capitalizations, such as, "LORD Jesus Christ!" We also adopted the original's change of font for all prayer passages which generally follow each of Moller's explanations and interpretations. This will enhance the visual recognition of prayers and *Sayings of Comfort* when reading and reciting them to those in need. We found it important to maintain a certain visual reference and *feel* of the original as readers would embark on their own *journeys* through the book.

Readers may forgive us for retaining the original's non-capitalization of pronouns referring to God –*he, him*– and also for observing the original's masculine pronoun –*he, him*– standing in for the singular antecedents: *human, human being,* or *person,* which naturally include both, women and men. We welcome readers' helpful suggestions for the presentation of future editions.

When translating Martin Moller's Scriptural quotations, we decided to keep to the German original. It had been suggested to apply uniformly the translation of the New Revised Standard Version, but we found the variations from Moller's 16[th]century sources to be quite distinctive, understanding also that standard translations into modern languages have pro-

gressed since Moller's era. For each Bible quote we offer a footnoted citation allowing readers to open their own preferred translation(s) for comparison; this was, in fact, an intended practice when reading *Erbauungsliteratur* –literary works of edification– of the time. We hope, thereby, to make this presentation of Moller's text more accessible for devotional readings by a variety of faith groups.

As for the citations of Scriptural passages, we decided to spell out the full name of each book of the Bible. The intent is to make finding the citations easier for less practiced readers of the Bible.

My son and I, as well as members of our team, had the privilege of applying some of the *Manuale's* passages as we experienced deaths in our own families. Witnessing the transition from fright into peace and from life into the blessed hour of death, our lives have changed forever. It is our sincere hope, dear reader, that you will find assurance in this book's prayers and simple words of comfort for your own life's journey.

Suzanne George

Introduction
by Austra Reinis

"It was my intention," writes Martin Moller (1547-1606) in the introduction to his *Handbook on Preparing to Die*, "... to bring such a book to light in which the common layperson would find not only the most important teaching, comfort, and exhortation, but also good, simple instruction on how to apply these to living a Christian life and to dying blessedly, in a loving, graceful, and comforting manner."[1] At the time Moller wrote this introduction on April 11, 1593, he had already published numerous other devotional works intended both to educate and to deepen the spiritual lives not only of his parishioners, but of a wider audience as well. The present translation of Moller's *Handbook*, in line with Moller's intentions, pursues a similar dual aim. First, it makes accessible to modern Christians and readers of English a German devotional classic which inspires reflection on suffering, mortality, and the Christian promise of divine forgiveness and everlasting life. Second, it makes available to general readers and historians of Christianity a text important to understanding German Lutheranism in the late sixteenth century.

Martin Moller's Life and Writings

Martin Moller was born in the village of Kropstädt, near Wittenberg, the year after Martin Luther's death. His parents were peasants of limited means. After some elementary schooling in Kropstädt, Moller attended the city school in Wittenberg. Unable to afford to study at the University of Wittenberg, he appears to have remained in town for some time as tutor in the home of the Deacon Petrus Etzelius. In 1566, when Moller was nineteen years old, a certain Johann Wels, then serving as member of the town council of Görlitz (today on Germany's

---

[1] Martin Moller, *Dear Soul: A Manual for the Rightful Art of Dying* (Bolivar, MO: Quiet Waters Publications, 2014), 203-204.

border with Poland), invited him to continue his secondary education at the well-known Gymnasium or secondary school at
Görlitz.[2] After two years of studies, one of his teachers, Lauren-
tius Ludovicus, a native of Löwenberg (today Lemberg in Poland), recommended him for the position of cantor, or music
teacher, at the school there. As cantor, Moller also did some
preaching in the local church. Four years later, in 1572, the
people of the nearby town of Kesselsdorff (Janowiec, Poland)
called him to be their pastor, despite the fact that he lacked
formal theological training. Prior to assuming the pastorate,
Moller traveled back to Wittenberg for his ordination. His ten-
ure in Kesselsdorff, however, lasted only twenty-seven weeks;
after that he returned to Löwenberg to assume the position of
city deacon (Stadt Diacon). Just over two years later, in 1575,
the city council of Sprottau (Szprotawa, Poland) called him to
serve as pastor in their church; there he remained for twenty-
five years. In 1600 he returned to Görlitz to take up the position
of head pastor (*pastor primarius*), which he held until his death
in 1606.[3]

During his tenures as pastor in Sprottau and Görlitz, Moller
appears to have dedicated significant time to writing. His first
two publications were translations from the original Greek and
Latin into German of three works of early church fathers: the
Letters of the Holy Martyr Ignatius, the *Dialogues of Theodoret*, and
several *Letters of Pope Leo the Great*. His selection of these works
for translation reflects the Christian humanist education he had

---

[2] Elke Axmacher, *Praxis Evangeliorum: Theologie und Frömmigkeit
bei Martin Moller (1547-1606)* (Göttingen: Vandenhoeck & Ruprecht,
1989), 22-23. Axmachers book is the most significant existing study of
Moller's life and literary works. For older biographical information
on Moller, see "Moller, Martin," in *Allgemeine Deutsche Biographie*, 22
(1885): 128, http://de.wikisource.org/wiki/ADB: Moller,_Martin; and
Stupperich, Robert, "Moller, Martin," in *Neue Deutsche Biographie* 18
(1997), 1, http://www.deutsche-biographie.de/pnd118870874.html,
both accessed 19. December 2013.

[3] Axmacher, *Praxis Evangeliorum*, 23-24.

received at Görlitz: The Christian humanists believed that true Christian teaching could best be recovered by studying the most ancient Christian writings. The fact that he dedicated his first translation to his congregation in Sprottau reveals that he wished to make learning otherwise available only to academics accessible also to Christian laypersons. Moller's desire to educate and spiritually edify his parishioners is evident also in his *Meditations of the Holy Fathers*. This work is a collection of texts and prayers written by early and medieval Christian writers, among them Augustine, Bernard of Clairvaux, Johannes Tauler, Cyprian, Jerome, and Anselm, gathered together and translated by Moller.[4]

Moller's first original work was his *Soliloquies Concerning the Passion of Jesus Christ* (1587). Both this work, and *The Birth of Jesus Christ* (1603), were dedicated to understanding Christ's incarnation and Christ's suffering, respectively, and to reflecting on how Christ's life, death, and resurrection benefits believers. Moller's *Great Mystery* (1595) reflects on the significance for Christians of the relationship with God that Christ made possible. Moller's most significant work is his *Practice of the Gospels* (1601); it is a complete collection of sermons on the gospel and epistle texts for each Sunday of the Christian year, beginning with the first Sunday in Advent, and ending with the twenty-seventh Sunday after Trinity Sunday. His *Treasure Trove of Prayers* (1603) is a collection of prayers excerpted from the *Practice of the Gospels*.[5] The desire to inform and to spiritually build up that is evident in the above works is also the motivating factor behind Moller's *Handbook on Preparing to Die* (1593), which deals with a significant aspect of the Christian life – the fact that all people must die – and teaches how Christians are to live in view of this reality.

---

[4] Axmacher, *Praxis Evangeliorum*, 91-92.
[5] Axmacher, *Praxis Evangeliorum*, 92-93.

Preparing for a Christian Death in Late Medieval and Reformation Germany

In the Middle Ages it was more difficult to avoid contact with death and dying than it is in the twenty-first century. Repeated waves of the plague killed not only adults, but children as well; women often died in childbirth; the infection of a small wound could have deadly consequences. Most people sought to die at home; people who died surrounded by family and loved ones considered themselves blessed.

The medieval church taught that dying persons ought to call for the spiritual assistance of their local priest. Surviving handbooks for priests, such as the *Rituale of Bishop Henry I. of Breslau* from the fourteenth century, show that sick persons were expected to confess their sins to their priest, who would then absolve them. Thereupon they received the sacraments of the eucharist, or communion, and the anointing of the sick. Psalms and prayers were spoken; the rituals were performed in Latin, the liturgical language of the medieval church.[6] Confession was the most important aspect of medieval preparation for death, because only persons who had confessed all of their mortal, that is, very serious sins could hope to escape eternal damnation. Moreover, the church taught that dying persons could not be certain of their eternal salvation. Even if they had remembered and confessed all their mortal sins, they could not know whether God had elevated them to a state of grace. And even if they had attained a state of grace, they could not be certain they would succeed in remaining in this state until the moment they died.[7]

Because eternal salvation was at stake at the moment of death, it was considered necessary for people to prepare to die

---

[6] Adolf Franz (ed.), *Das Rituale des Bischofs Heinrich I. von Breslau* (Freiburg im Breisgau: Herder, 1912), 32-39.

[7] Sven Grosse, *Heilsungewißheit und Scrupulositas im späten Mittelalter: Studien zu Johannes Gerson und Gattungen der Frömmigkeitstheologie seiner Zeit* (Tübingen: J. C. B. Mohr (Paul Siebeck), 1994), 35-41.

while they were still in good health. Clergy thought it wise to teach Christian laypersons to minister to the dying, given that, especially at times of plague, priests were either dead so busy they were unable to attend every deathbed. To assist with this, theologians and clergy devised a variety of self-help books and handbooks known by the Latin term *ars moriendi*, or art of dying. One of the most widely-disseminated of these books was the anonymous *Art of Dying Well* (*Speculum artis bene moriendi*) (1414-18). Originally written in Latin, it circulated in manuscript before the invention of the printing press, and was translated into several languages, including English. This book consisted of a variety of sections: Instructions to caregivers in the form of exhortations to dying persons to faith and confession, questions to ask of dying persons about their faith, prayers to be said with and by the dying, instructions on how dying persons were to face the demonic temptations they could expect on their deathbed, and a series of concluding prayers.[8] A condensed version of the *Art of Dying Well*, consisting of the exhortations, the demonic temptations illustrated with vivid woodcuts, and a series of concluding admonitions to prayer along with prayer texts was also published in a variety of languages, including German, but not English. The five demonic temptations it taught dying Christians to resist were to doubt their faith, to despair of their salvation, to fail to be patient in suffering, to believe they deserved salvation on account of all their good works, and to regret leaving behind their wealth.[9] It was important to learn to expect and resist these temptations, be-

---

[8] Mary Catharine O'Connor, *The Art of Dying Well: The Development of the Ars moriendi* (New York: AMS Press, 1966), 7-10; for an English translation of the text, see *The boke of the craft of dying*, in *Yorkshire Writers: Richard Rolle of Hampole and his Followers*, vol. 2, ed. C. Horstman (London: Swan Sonnenschein, 1896), 406-20.

[9] O'Connor, *The Art of Dying Well*, 9; for a reprint of a beautiful German woodcut edition see Ernst Weil, ed., *Die deutsche Übersetzung der Ars moriendi des Meisters Ludwig von Ulm um 1470* (facsimile reprint, Munich-Pasing, 1922).

cause the person who gave in to any one of them would face eternity in hell.

With the advent of the Lutheran Reformation, the genre of the *ars moriendi* underwent a radical theological transformation. Martin Luther rejected the traditional teaching that Christians could not be certain of their eternal salvation. On the contrary, he taught that Christians could rest assured of their salvation, and that this assurance could be attained through faith in God's gracious promise to forgive sins. This teaching, which came to be known as justification by faith, became the basis for Lutheran teaching on preparing for death.

Martin Luther himself wrote the first "Lutheran" contribution to the *ars moriendi* genre, entitled *Sermon on Preparing to Die* (1519). Following tradition, Luther taught that dying persons were to draw up a will, to seek reconciliation with loved ones and neighbors, and to receive the traditional deathbed sacraments. In his exhortation to confession, however, Luther broke with tradition; he instructed dying persons to confess not all of their sins, but only the serious sins which lay most heavily on their conscience.[10] The remainder of the sermon consisted of instruction on the meaning of the deathbed sacraments. These are best understood, Luther writes, when one recognizes that they help one overcome the demonic temptations. Luther speaks of these temptations as images of death, sin, and hell; they correspond to the late medieval temptation of despair of salvation. Luther teaches that the images or temptations can be overcome by meditating on Christ's passion. When Christians are tempted to despair of salvation on account of the certainty of impending death, the gravity of their sins, or the fear of damnation, they are to contemplate the death of Christ on the

---

[10] Austra Reinis, *Reforming the Art of Dying: The ars moriendi in the German Reformation (1519-1528)* (Aldershot, Great Britain: Ashgate, 1997), 50-52. For an English translation of Luther's text, see Martin Luther, *A Sermon on Preparing to Die* (1519), in *Luther's Works, American Edition*, ed. Jaroslav Pelikan et al., 42:99-115.

cross, through which their own death and sin are defeated and eternal life is given to them. In conclusion, Luther encourages dying persons to receive the deathbed sacraments joyfully, and to trust in the certainty of salvation that is Christ's gift. Thus Luther draws on motifs found in traditional *ars moriendi* works, but rejects their central teaching – that dying Christians cannot be certain of their salvation.[11]

Luther's colleagues and successors followed in Luther's footsteps, teaching and consoling the Christians entrusted to their spiritual care with numerous contributions to the *ars moriendi* genre. In the sixteenth century alone, over a hundred such booklets were published, Martin Moller's *Handbook* (1593) among them.[12] Three themes recur with particular frequency in these works, all three of them already present in Luther's *Sermon on Preparing to Die*: 1.Instruction on how to fend off deathbed temptation, 2.consolation in the form of instruction on the meaning of the sacraments of baptism and communion, and 3.exhortation to meditation on Christ's passion.[13] With the passage of time, the handbooks for ministry to the dying became ever more voluminous and comprehensive, containing formulas for "greetings, individual addresses geared to various kinds of people, formulas of confession of varying length, Bible verses with commentary, hymn stanzas, commented prayers, blessings, exhortations to persons present, and much more."[14]

---

[11] Reinis, *Reforming the Art of Dying*, 47.

[12] For an extensive bibliography of sixteenth-century German Lutheran works in the *ars moriendi* genre, see Luise Schottroff, *Die Bereitung zum Sterben: Studien zu den frühen reformatorischen Sterbebüchern* (Göttingen: Vandenhoeck & Ruprecht, 2012), 107-34.

[13] Reinis, *Reforming the Art of Dying*, 250-53.

[14] Claudia Resch, *Trost im Angesicht des Todes: Frühe reformatorische Anleitungen zur Seelsorge and Kranken und Sterbenden* (Tübingen and Basel: A. Francke, 2006), 209.

Martin Moller's Handbook on Preparing to Die

While in its choice of themes Moller's *Handbook* bears considerable resemblance to the late medieval *Art of Dying Well*, in its theology it preserves Martin Luther's theme of the joyful certainty of salvation. The nine chapters of Moller's book treat, respectively, the topics of 1.Contemplating human mortality; 2.Preparing for a blessed death with daily confession of sins; 3.Leading a Christian life; 4.Conducting oneself appropriately when afflicted with illness; 5.Dealing with temptations; 6.Surrendering to death joyfully; 7.Confronting the torment of dying and the ugliness of death; 8.Finding Scripture verses, prayers, hymns, and formulas for commending the dying person's soul to God; 9.Knowing the eternal bliss or eternal damnation that awaits those who have died.

In its approach to these themes, Moller's book is quite different from the earliest Lutheran handbooks on dying: It is not a sermon or series of sermons on preparing to die; nor is it primarily a handbook for caregivers helping the dying, although it can be used as such. Instead, it is a guide to prayer and meditation for individual Christians who wish to contemplate their own mortality, and in doing so, grow closer to God, lead a better Christian life, and prepare to die a Christian death. In his introduction, as cited above, Moller emphasizes that his intention is not only to provide his readers with good Christian teaching, but also to show them how to apply the teaching to reap spiritual benefit. Such application takes place primarily by means of prayer. In the third section of his first chapter, for example, Moller asks: "What does it mean to die blessedly?" Alluding to several New Testament passages, he teaches: "To die blessedly means to conclude one's life in the right and true faith, to commend one's soul to the Lord Jesus Christ, and – with a heartfelt desire for eternal bliss – to fall asleep gently and joyously, and to depart from here (Lk 2[:29]; Phil 1[:23]; 1 Tim 4[:6])." He then provides a prayer, likewise rooted in Scripture, which explicitly reinforces the preceding teaching: "LORD Jesus Christ! you alone know my hour: I pray you, give me a blessed ending and thereupon take my soul into your hands. Amen!" (Mt 6:[10, 33]; Ac 7[:59]).[15] In contrast to the authors of the earliest Lutheran handbooks on dying, for Moller, Christian teaching and the application of Christian teaching to the life of the individual believer are two distinct, albeit closely related concerns.[16]

While Moller agrees with the biblical, medieval, and early Reformation understanding of death as God's just punishment for human sin, a punishment which is to be obediently accepted in faith, his teaching on dying reflects a broader shift in cultural attitudes toward death that had taken place since the Reformation. To a greater extent than in the early Reformation, in Moller's day, popular culture had come to place greater value on earthly life and its enjoyments, and had come to perceive death as unnatural, and therefore a threat to life.[17] In the fifth chapter, Moller acknowledges such changed perceptions toward life and death, and treats them, if not as sins, nevertheless as temptations to be overcome. Speaking of the human tendency to fear death, he writes: "That is natural, dear soul, for our nature has initially been created not for death, but for life." After all, as Moller points out, Jesus, too, feared death. In the prayer that reinforces this teaching, however, Moller brings together the theme of fear of natural death with the traditional teaching that death is a deserved punishment for sin:[18] "I thank you, Lord Jesus Christ! that you have not created me for death, but for life, and that you engraved in my heart the love for life. I ask you from the bottom of my heart, teach me to keep in mind that death reigns over me for the sake of sins, and that death will finally strangle me. . . . Do help me, that I cling to

---

[15] Moller, *Dear Soul: A Manual for the Rightful Art of Dying*, 32.

[16] Axmacher, *Praxis Evangeliorum*, 203.

[17] Axmacher, *Praxis Evangeliorum*, 204.

[18] Axmacher, *Praxis Evangeliorum*, 204-205.

you steadfastly with true faith – my Lord! who is life itself -- , that I overcome all fear of death . . . (Jn 11[:25-26])".[19]

Given that death is the divine punishment for sin, forgiveness, that is, justification is the ultimate religious comfort that Moller, like Luther, offers his readers.[20] Also like Luther, the consolation Moller offers is permeated with the conviction that penitent sinners can be certain of divine forgiveness: "Yes, I know and I believe, I trust and I am certain, my Redeemer, . . . that your descent into hell is my rescue from the force of hell and of the devil; . . . and that your ascension to heaven is my assurance that I am a certain heir of eternal life, and that through you I have heaven already within me."[21] Moller, however, goes a step beyond Luther in offering comfort in the promise of mystical union with God. This comfort is also expressed in a prayer:[22] "You [Jesus] are within me, and I am within you; everything that is yours is also mine, namely, life, and eternal delight and joy. . . . When I have you, then I have everything that pleases me, here, temporally, and there, eternally."[23]

An Enduring Devotional Classic

It seems likely that Moller's realistic acknowledgment of human attitudes toward and feelings about death, his skill in clearly articulating Christian teaching, and his ability to merge human experience and Christian teaching in heartfelt, yet informed prayers contributed to the lasting popularity of the volume. The *Handbook* was published in at least eight editions in Moller's lifetime, all of them in Görlitz, and in another twenty or so editions before the end of the seventeenth century, not only in Görlitz, but also in cities as far away as Nuremberg and

---

[19] Moller, *Dear Soul: A Manual for the Rightful Art of Dying*, 104.

[20] Axmacher, *Praxis Evangeliorum*, 206.

[21] Moller, *Dear Soul: A Manual for the Rightful Art of Dying*, 43.

[22] Axmacher, *Praxis Evangeliorum*, 207.

[23] Moller, *Dear Soul: A Manual for the Rightful Art of Dying*, 121.

Basel. A French translation appeared in 1619 in Oppenheim, and was reprinted in Bern in 1669.[24] By around 1808 Moller's book had made it across the Atlantic Ocean to Lebanon, Pennsylvania, where it was published, still in German, by Jacob Schnee with the title *Anweisung zum Christlichen Leben und seligen Sterben*.[25] It is the hope of the collaborators on this English translation that Moller's book will continue to find devoted readers on this side of the Atlantic.

Austra Reinis
Springfield, Missouri

---

[24] Cf. *Verzeichnis der im deutschen Sprachbereich erschienenen Drucke des 16. Jahrhunderts* (VD 16) and *Verzeichnis der im deutschen Sprachraum Erschienenen Drucke des 17. Jahrhunderts* (VD 17), both at www.gateway-bayern.de/index_vd16.html; accessed March 11, 2014. This database of sixteenth- and seventeenth-century imprints is continually updated.

[25] Cf. the *Karlsruhe Virtual Catalog* at *www.ubka.uni-karlsruhe .de/kvk_en.html*, accessed March 11, 2014.

Editor's Note

Shortly before I began working on this text, there was a loss in my family. Martin Moller's words on preparing oneself for death, therefore, became more immediate and resonant to me than they may have been otherwise. I hope that, like me, the reader finds in this work a clear-eyed appraisal of death and the meaning it gives to life. Moller has sounded a voice lacking in the clatter of day-to-day routine.

I would like to thank Suzanne George for including me on this project, for her vision for bringing Moller's words to press, and for her steadfast belief that this is a message for our time. Thanks to Dr. Stephen Trobisch for listening when I needed a second opinion on matters of language and for providing much-needed background knowledge in how moveable type was set, which often proved invaluable when trying to locate scriptural references. I also would like to thank Dr. David Trobisch, who assisted many times when my own Biblical knowledge was simply inadequate.

Finally, I would like to thank my parents, Michael and Cindy Perryman, for their genuine enthusiasm in getting the smallest details of written language right—particularly when that language conveys a matter of faith. I have inherited their sense of grammatical urgency, which I hope has served this text well.

Sheila Perryman

MANUALE
DE

PRÆPARATIONE
AD MORTEM.

that is:
a special manual
for the salutary

Death — Preparation.
derived from God's Word
by

MARTIN MOLLER
formerly of the Christian congregation at Görlitz,
the Head Pastor

S T A D E.
printed and published by Caspar Holwein.

Contents

Prologue by Suzanne George 7

Introduction by Austra Reinis 11

Contents 25

The 1ˢᵗ Chapter. 31

Summarizes the content of the book and contemplates that we human beings are not only mortal, but also quite uncertain about when, how, and where God would claim us from this world. 31

I. Tell me in a brief summary: what must I –from God's Word and from all sermons– learn, retain, and do? 31

II. What is a Christian life indeed? 31

III. What does it mean to die blessedly? 32

IV. Must we humans all die? 32

V. If only God, the Lord, would have revealed to us the hour of our death, so that we can get ready and prepare at the right time. 33

VI. How shall I, in my simple-mindedness, rightly consider these four articles? 34

    1ˢᵗ Tempus (Time) 34

    2ⁿᵈ Locus (Place) 35

    3ʳᵈ Status (State) 35

    4ᵗʰ Modus (Manner) 36

The 2ⁿᵈ Chapter. 39

Teaches the right and salutary art of dying, and contemplates the three articles of true Christian penance. 39

I. Since we are never safe from death, it is necessary that both, the young and old, the short and tall, the rich and poor remain meticulously watchful every day and learn the rightful and blessed art of dying. 39

II. How shall I prepare for a blessed death? 40

III. What is rightful, true Christian penance? 41

IV. Explain to me the three articles of true penance, and give me instruction how I shall submit myself to it and practice it daily. 42

The first article of true penance. 42

V. Shall a person in such grief dispair and in sin become dejected? 45

The second article of true penance. 45

VI. Since I am now completely reconciled with God through Christ, made just before him through faith, and saved with hope even now, may I then behave as I wish until my dying hour arrives? 51

The third article of true penance. 51

VII. Is it sufficient if a person does rightful penance only for one time, or only once a year? 54

The 3rd Chapter...57

Summarizes six distinguished articles that belong to a Christian life delightful to God..57

I. When I commence with daily penance, and when I encounter much adversity on this narrow track, how shall I behave so that my faith does not end and that I do not go astray?..............................57

II. Explain to me these six articles, so that I understand them well, and that I abide by them throughout my lifetime. 58

1st The word of God. The first article belonging to a Christian life......58

2nd Baptism. The second article belonging to a Christian life..............63

3rd The Lord's Supper. The third article belonging to a Christian life..65

4th The daily cross and suffering of the children of God. The fourth article belonging to a Christian life...71

The 1st rule of the cross. 72

The 2nd rule of the cross. 73

The 3rd rule of the cross. 74

The 4th rule of the cross. 74

The 5th rule of the cross. 75

The 6th rule of the cross. 76

The 7th rule of the cross. 77

5th A Christian's outward vocation. The fifth article belonging to a Christian life..78

6th Daily prayer. The sixth article belonging to a Christian life.........82

The 4th Chapter...87

Describes how a Christian shall conduct himself when God afflicts him with illness...87

I. How shall a Christian conduct himself when he becomes ill?............87

II. Explain to me now the aforementioned nine articles, so that I will properly learn how to behave in my illness. 89

1st Illnesses are God's rods. 89

2nd Penance is the soul's health..91

3rd One shall ask God for rescue...92

4th Proper care is not to be disregarded................................93

5th Patience is a precious herb in illness. 94

6th Comfort in prolonged illness...95

7th Temptation. 96

8th, 9th Death or Life. 99

The 5th Chapter. 103

Gives an account of various worldly and carnal notions which may arise and which may often become quite burdensome in the daily practice of the art of dying. 103

I. Whenever contemplating the hour of death, whether in illness or in health, a Christian's human heart will naturally become frightened of death. 103

II. One still finds many people with a yearning desire for death. 104

III. May a person pray for a longer life with a good conscience? 105

IV. By which motivation shall every single person surrender willingly to dying? 107

V. This world is nevertheless fair, and its course is beautiful; who would not rather want to stay here. 108

VI. No matter the circumstance, for him, who owns money and estate, who dwells in honor and glory, who lives in pleasure and joy, it will be difficult to leave everything behind when he shall depart. 110

VII. It will be painful when a woman must leave her beloved husband, or a man his beloved wife and children, who are often left in poverty, without real trade and secure provisions. 111

VIII. Say whatever you want, life is noble, life is endearing. 114

The 6th Chapter. 119

Gives an account of how a Christian can and shall surrender joyfully and cheerfully to dying, overcome all bitterness of death, and endure in faithful steadfastness until the end. 119

I. Tell me now, how should and how may I silence the fear of death, so that I will surrender joyfully and cheerfully to my God? 119

II. This will indeed bring life and comfort into the heart; if only I could also persevere steadfastly, so that my faith will endure. 122

III. What shall a Christian do if he does not always find such joyousness of faith, but instead great weakness, concern, and agitation, often questioning whether or not he is chosen for salvation? 125

The 7th Chapter. 131

Considers several beautiful contemplations in which the faithful heart will find comfort regarding the hideous image of the deceased body, the unfriendliness of the grave, and the gasping and twitching of the dying; so that at last the faithful heart will find refuge within the healing remedy of God and neither taste the bitterness nor feel the thorn of death. 131

I. It is indeed manifest that a human will die. 131

II. Death does make us abominable and hideous, cold and misshapen; we must grow stiff, and waste away in the grave. 132

III. Frightening things must be considered, the taste of which I dare not even imagine: death, dying, grave, tomb, being interred, being covered up, decaying, decomposing..134

IV. I hear you say all this; but when I observe how humans die, I see them suffering, indeed; for several of them tremble, twitch, gasp, turn their eyes, sweat in fear. 136

V. Is there no medicine which one may take to make the sting of death be felt and tasted less severely?..137

The 8th Chapter...141

Conveys many beautiful verses from Holy Scripture, as well as several devotional prayers and lamentations, which shall be recited for the dying; this chapter also conveys how the bystanders shall behave who witness the departure and who have given care to the deceased person. 141

I. Do provide me now with several verses from Holy, Godly Scripture, so that I become familiar with them, that I find comfort in them at my end, and that I may restore my soul..141
Articles of Faith...141

II. Teach me also several short prayers which will restore me on my deathbed, and which I may recite also to others who are dying. 149

III. Some patients also like to hear songs: which of them shall be sung to them?..159

IV. Do also provide me with some short lamentations which may be applied when the ill person is very weak, has light breath, cannot speak; particularly such verses which commend his soul to God. 161

V. What shall the bystanders do when they see that a Christian has bid farewell, has been comforted until the end, and has passed away blessedly?..164

The 9th Chapter...167

Describes where the mortal souls will arrive after their departure and in which condition. It also contemplates the resurrection of our bodies, the joy of eternal bliss, and the pain of eternal damnation. 167

I. Since the souls are immortal, where do they go, and how will they fare when they depart from the bodies?..167

II. Will the dear souls —since they know that their remains decay so pitifully in the cold earth— yearn for their bodies; and will time seem long to them since the day of judgment and the resurrection of the body will be drawn out?...170

III. Therefore believe assuredly that these bodies of ours will rise from the dead and will live eternally together with their souls...................172

IV. For all of humanity, eternal life will indeed be a gloriously joyous life. 177

V. Where, however, will the ungodly end up, and how will they fare?.....184

Appendix..188
Preface by Martin Moller...189
Epilogue by Suzanne George...................................207
Endorsements 211

The salutary and most useful contemplation

of how a human being shall learn from God's Word
to live in a Christian manner and
to die blessedly.

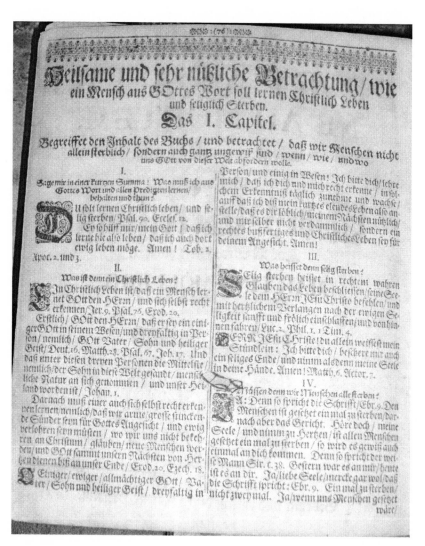

The 1st Chapter.

Summarizes the content of the book and contemplates that we human beings are not only mortal, but also quite uncertain about when, how, and where God would claim us from this world.

I.

Tell me in a brief summary: what must I –from God's Word and from all sermons– learn, retain, and do?

 You shall learn to live in a Christian manner and to die blessedly.[1]

Oh, help me, my God! help me so that I may learn to live here in such a way, so that I may also live there eternally. Amen![2]

II.

What is a Christian life indeed?

A Christian life is established when a human being learns to know God, the Lord, and to know himself rightly.[3]

Firstly, know the Lord God, that he is one God in three persons, namely, God the Father, the Son, and the Holy Spirit.[4] And that among these three persons, the middle one, namely, the Son, has been sent into this world, has assumed human nature, and has become our savior.[5]

Next, one must also learn to know oneself rightly, namely, that we are poor, great, and reeking sinners in the sight of God,

---

[1] Psalm 90; Ecclesiastes 12.
[2] Tobias 2; Revelation 2 and 3.
[3] Jeremiah 9; Psalm 76; Exodus 20.
[4] Deuteronomy 16; Matthew 28; Psalm 67; John 17.
[5] John 1.

and that we would be eternally lost if we did not convert to Christ, believe in him, become new human beings, and serve God and our neighbor with our whole hearts until our end.⁶

Only, eternal, almighty God, Father, Son, and Holy Spirit, three persons and one being! I pray you, teach me to know you and my own self rightly, to gain such knowledge daily and grow, so that I orient my short, miserable life in such a way that it will glorify you, that it will serve my neighbor, and that it will not be condemning to myself, but that it will be a righteous, penitent, and Christian life in your sight. Amen!

III.

What does it mean to die blessedly?

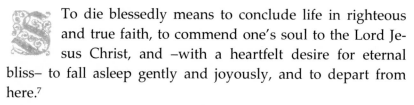 To die blessedly means to conclude life in righteous and true faith, to commend one's soul to the Lord Jesus Christ, and –with a heartfelt desire for eternal bliss– to fall asleep gently and joyously, and to depart from here.⁷

LORD Jesus Christ! you alone know my hour: I pray you, give me a blessed ending and thereupon take my soul into your hands. Amen!⁸

IV.

Must we humans all die?

Yes, for thus speaks scripture, HUMANS ARE DESTINED TO DIE ONCE; THEN, HOWEVER, FOLLOWS THE JUDGMENT.⁹ Do listen, my soul, and take to heart that all humans are predetermined to die at once; thus, death will certainly also come to you at one time. For the wise man says, YESTERDAY IT WAS UP TO ME; TODAY IT IS UP TO YOU.¹⁰ Yes, dear

---

⁶ Exodus 20; Ezekiel 18.

⁷ Luke 2; Philippians 1; 1ˢᵗ Timothy 4.

⁸ Matthew 6; Acts 7.

⁹ Hebrews 9:27.

¹⁰ Sirach 38:22.

soul, keep well in mind what scripture says: TO DIE ONCE,[11] and not twice. Indeed, if we humans had been destined to die twice, then someone, if he had not died well the first time, would die better the second time: but no, dying badly once will bring eternal perdition.

Lord, my God! do teach me that there must be an end with me, and that my life has a goal, and that I will have to depart; BEHOLD, MY DAYS ARE A HAND'S BREADTH TO YOU, AND MY LIFE IS LIKE NOTHING TO YOU.[12] My God, TEACH ME TO BEAR IN MIND THAT I MUST DIE, SO THAT I BECOME PRUDENT,[13] and that I learn the right and beneficial art of dying. Amen!

V.

If only God, the Lord, would have revealed to us the hour of our death, so that we can get ready and prepare at the right time.

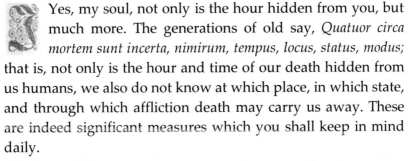 Yes, my soul, not only is the hour hidden from you, but much more. The generations of old say, *Quatuor circa mortem sunt incerta, nimirum, tempus, locus, status, modus;* that is, not only is the hour and time of our death hidden from us humans, we also do not know at which place, in which state, and through which affliction death may carry us away. These are indeed significant measures which you shall keep in mind daily.

You holy and wise GOD! how completely are your thoughts not our thoughts, and your ways not our ways; but as much as the sky is far above the earth, so are your paths far above our paths, and your

---

[11] Hebrews 9:27.

[12] Psalm 39:5.

[13] Psalm 90:12.

thoughts far above our thoughts.[14] Grant me to step in front of you daily with heartfelt assurance, to pray for a blessed hour of dying, and to have the firm faith that you will expose me only to what is beneficial, good, and blissful for me. Amen![15]

VI.

How shall I, in my simple-mindedness, rightly consider these four measures?

1ˢᵗ Tempus (Time)

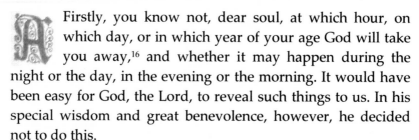 Firstly, you know not, dear soul, at which hour, on which day, or in which year of your age God will take you away,[16] and whether it may happen during the night or the day, in the evening or the morning. It would have been easy for God, the Lord, to reveal such things to us. In his special wisdom and great benevolence, however, he decided not to do this.

For behold, my soul, we miserable humans have been spoiled by sin, and we are so fond of our worldly existence that –if we knew the hour of our death– we would not commemorate God very much; we would neither fear him, nor love him, nor pray to him, nor do any penance until the predetermined hour of our death would have arrived. If one would do penance only at that time, many would not have learned what rightful penance is, and they would remain ill-prepared. For this reason, it is surely not harmful for us humans, but beneficial and well, that we do not know the hour of our departure.

Oh, my God, how those humans are nothing at all who seem to live so securely.[17] Truly, the human, born by woman, lives only for a short time and is filled with disquiet. He blooms like a flower, takes flight

---

[14] Isaiah 55.

[15] Romans 8.

[16] Sirach 38.

[17] Psalm 39.

like a shadow, and does not last.[18] He has his designated time; the number of moons stands with you; you have set a goal for him which he will not exceed.[19] My God, who has concealed the time of my death, according to your wise counsel, help me that I live not a single day without true penance. My Lord, who has concealed the lone hour of my departure, grant me to conduct my entire life so that I will be found in rightful Christian readiness day and night, even at every hour and any moment. Amen!

2nd Locus (Place)

Secondly, you do not know at which place you may find your end bestowed on you, whether you pass away at home or in a strange place, whether in your bed or in the field. Indeed, my soul, the pointer of our life's clock never stands still, and no human knows when it will stop. Thus, death is pursuing us, and he keeps at our heels; he takes us away wherever he finds us; he awaits you at every place. If you are a prudent servant, do await death everywhere with a prepared, penitent heart.[20]

Oh, my God, let me become aware that at all places am I a miserable, mortal human being, and that nowhere am I safe from death. Since he is out to get me, and since he lingers everywhere, so help that I become a prudent servant, and that I guardedly await him at all places with a penitent heart. Amen![21]

3rd Status (State)

Thirdly, you also do not know, my soul, in which condition the Lord your God may find you, whether he may find you sleeping or waking, happy or sad, in worldly or in spiritual affairs, drunk or sober, angry or peaceful. Oh, dear soul, do become diligently aware of yourself, and do not let yourself be found in such a state in which you would not willingly like to die. For

---

[18] Job 14:1-2.
[19] Job 15:5.
[20] Matthew 24.
[21] Matthew 24.

Sirach says, REMEMBER THAT DEATH DOES NOT TARRY,[22] so be well aware what kind of a bond you have with death. Yes, dear soul, as the Lord will find you, so will he also judge you.[23]

Guard me, my Lord Jesus, from being overly confident so that I do not live mindlessly into the day like the ungodly who have no hope.[24] Grant me, instead, that –day and night– I live in such a way, and that I am found in all my doing to be prepared at every moment so that I may take a blessed farewell. Amen!

4ᵗʰ Modus (Manner)

Fourthly, you do also not know, dear soul, by which illness your God will let you die, whether you will perish through pestilence, through illness in the head, through fever or ulcers or consumption, whether you will perish by drowning or by burning, through murder or wild animals, or suchlike. Yes, my soul, many say, "When I get ill, I will do penance, and then I will prepare myself." This person, however, does not know whether he would be so fortunate for God to let him have an illness. Do we not encounter such examples every day? How many a red mouth has paled –while commemorating God– by suffering a sudden stroke or another fatal punishment before becoming ill?

My God! how imprudent we miserable and careless humans are indeed. A bird is an irrational animal, and yet, when it sees that the one next to it has been hit and shot away, it swerves off in a hurry. Yes, when it sees a person drawing the bow and aiming at it, it does not wait, but it soars away to a place of safety. Oh, dear soul, so shall we humans also act; we encountering such examples every day: death does not take a break, but he shoots at one heart after the other, bringing them down. Oh, get ready, my soul, and fly away from sin toward righteousness, away from hell toward heaven, away from the terrible,

---

[22] Sirach 14:12a.

[23] Luke 18.

[24] 1ˢᵗ Thessalonians 4.

disdainful world toward your Lord Jesus Christ, so that you can indeed say with comfort, "Go ahead and shoot, death, if you like; for even if you bring down my mortal heart and end the limited time of my life, I –in right faith– still have the governor of eternal life with me and in me; he gives me more than you can take from me."

Therefore, dear soul, do not hold back on penance since you still can sin; do not profess to become pious, and do not anticipate your life's betterment until death comes.[25]

Lord Jesus, my savior! safeguard me from painful illnesses and from a terrible death. Do not assail me in my sins, and let me not die without penitence. Instead, convey to me a quiet, soft end without great fright and pain, so that –keeping my good senses– I may *make* a good end with a good mind, that I avow your name until my departure, and that I commend my soul into your hands devoutly and wholeheartedly. Amen!

---

[25] Sirach 18

The 2nd Chapter.

**Teaches the right and salutary art of dying, and
contemplates the three articles of
true Christian penance.**

I.

**Since we are never safe from death, it is necessary that both,
the young and the old, the short and the tall, the rich and
the poor remain meticulously watchful every day and
learn the rightful and blessed art of dying.**

 Truly, this is taught to us by everyday examples. And Sirach says, REMEMBER HIM, AS HE HAS DIED, SO WILL YOU HAVE TO DIE ALSO. YESTERDAY IT WAS UP TO ME, TODAY IT IS UP TO YOU.[1] And elsewhere he says, TODAY A KING, TOMORROW DEAD.[2] Indeed, dear soul, death is like a reaper in the meadow taking down everything with the sickle; he does not care whether it is a little blade of grass or a small flower, an herb or a rose; he also does not ask how old, how beautiful, how tasty it is. Likewise does death; no one is too strong for him and no one too young, no castle is too high and no fortress too strong. Nor will he be turned away with money or gold. Indeed, if you could give all the world's goods to him, you will not be able to purchase from him a single hour by which he would delay and add at your pleasure. Everyone shall bear this in mind daily and, indeed, take it to heart; no one shall softly lay down his head at night until he has learned the blessed art of dying – rightly and well. Oh, my God! how the human being is equal to nothing![3] How his time and all his glory is fleeting away like a shadow, not knowing whether he shall die young

---

[1] Sirach 38:22.
[2] Sirach 10:10.
[3] Psalm 144.

or old, and safeguarding himself against death neither with force nor with wealth.

Help me, my God, to take this to heart from my earliest youth onward, to walk my path without blemish, and to orient myself according to your word.[4] Govern me through your Holy Spirit, so that my heart does not go amiss, and that I rely neither on my youth, my health, and my strength, nor on my honor, my wealth, and my beauty; grant me to consider well the main design of all teachings and commandments every day:[5] fear God and keep his commandments. For this pertains to all humans: God will bring all deeds to judgment – which is concealed– whether they be good or evil. My God! etch this into my heart and grant me not only to know that, but also to act and to orient myself accordingly until my end. Amen!

II.
How shall I prepare for a blessed death?

 The right preparation for a blessed ending is a daily, Christian, penitent life. If you intend to die well and blessedly, dear soul, so do righteous, true penance, and persist in it until the end. For scripture says, GOD WILL ACCEPT PENANCE OF SINS.[6] And scripture also says, WHOEVER PERSISTS TO THE END, HE WILL DIE BLESSEDLY.[7]

Praise to you, my God, that you do not take pleasure in our death and damnation, but that you intend for us to convert and to live![8] Help me, my Lord Jesus, that I do not delay my conversion toward you, and that I do not postpone my penitence until tomorrow![9] For you did

---

[4] Psalm 119.
[5] Ecclesiastes 12.
[6] Wisdom 12:19b.
[7] Matthew 24:13.
[8] Ezekiel 18 and 33.
[9] Sirach 5.

assure me of your mercy; however, you did not promise me another morning of a new day. Ah, grant me to do penitence today and become converted so that tomorrow I will not be caught up in my sins, and be consumed.[10] Amen.

III.
What is rightful, true Christian penance?

 Penance is nothing other than when a person refrains from sin and becomes wholeheartedly converted to God.

Which is stated in these three
articles:

1. Firstly, that a human recognizes his sin, and that he does heartfelt penance.

2. Secondly, that he does not despair in his sins, but that he believes in Jesus Christ, who has paid for our sins, and that he finds heartfelt joy and comfort in Jesus.

3. Thirdly, that he also proves his faith with daily renewed obedience toward God and toward humans.

Lord, my God! I know that I can neither attain true penitence by my own reason and strength, nor believe in my Lord Jesus Christ. I pray you, stir my heart through your Holy Spirit, and grant that my conversion be not hypocrisy, that my faith be not untrue but righteous and heartfelt,[11] and that it be perceived and known at all times by its righteous fruits.[12] Amen!

---

[10] Psalm 95.
[11] Sirach 1.
[12] Matthew 3.

IV.

Explain to me the three articles of true penance, and give me instruction how I shall submit myself to it and practice it daily.

The first article of true penance.

 Gladly. The first article is rightful, true remorse and agony about the sin. For, without cognizance of the sin, faith is only hypocrisy, and it is not righteous. Hence, learn to recognize your sin, contemplate God's anger toward sin, and repent wholeheartedly in this manner:

O my Lord Jesus! how my heart becomes frightened when I think about the day of my death. My God, how my soul is scared when I behold the day of the terrible judgment because I am not safe from death for one moment; I also do not know at which hour you may put me before your solemn judgment.[13]

Oh, how utterly my heart is tainted, how severely I have sinned! My Lord, behold, there I have your holy ten commandments in front of my eyes, even in my conscience, and I know that they are the law of your eternal justice, and that they show me the articles by which I shall conform to your holy will so as not to lose my blessedness. Oh, dreadful perdition! Oh, hideous deterioration of all my strengths; also, the great damage caused by Adam's fall, which we all have inherited! My God! how utterly my heart fails to conform to your commandments.

I certainly recognize and feel that I was conceived and born in original sin, that I have been begotten of sinful semen, and that MY MOTHER HAS CONCEIVED ME IN SIN.[14] My entire being is sick,[15] MY WHOLE HEART IS DIM, EVEN FROM THE SOLES OF MY FEET TO THE TOP OF MY

---

[13] Matthew 24.
[14] Psalm 51:5b.
[15] Isaiah 1.

HEAD THERE IS NOTHING HEALTHY,[16] nothing righteous on me; instead, all is decayed through the sin which lives in me.[17] Fie, you devil, you hellish murderer; how pitiably you have marred me; my sanity you have darkened, my will reversed, my heart and all my strength ruined.

My God! I confess, I know, I feel that within me –that is, in my flesh– nothing good resides;[18] instead, everything is full of sinful wounds, of sores and bruises, and of abscessed boils.[19] And even if I had never carried out or committed a sin all my life, so would I still be a child of wrath because of the original sin, for which alone I would be damned and ostracized before your sight.

Sadly, however, more was added to the original sin; for –from my youth onward–[20] I have transgressed all of your ten commandments, I have never kept any of them! My tainted nature disabled me from keeping them; I have, instead, sinned against the greatest and the least, gravely and terribly, with sinful desires, sinful cravings, sinful gestures, sinful thoughts, sinful words and deeds, sinful silence and negligence against you, my dear, pious God, and against my neighbor. I know and also understand that no sin is too small, no misdeed too meager –even if it involved merely a thought– not to have earned eternal death and eternal damnation.

I also worry that many terrible sins are still hidden from me; indeed, many of those in my youth,[21] of which I am unaware now, and which I now regard not as sins but as good deeds: all these will be rightly revealed to me thereafter; they will bear their right color –being coal-black– and will attack me like in an ambush.

What shall I do? Where shall I go? My God, if you enter into judgment with me, then I must be eternally cast out from your presence.[22]

---

[16] Isaiah 1:5b-6a.

[17] Romans 5.

[18] Romans 7.

[19] Isaiah 1:6.

[20] Psalm 25.

[21] Psalm 25.

[22] Psalm 143.

Oh, my dear soul, you barren tree, oh, you dry, useless wood – you are worthy of being cut off and thrown into the eternal fire.[23] Oh, you lost son, you wayward child, how you have turned away from your pious Father, and how you fed with the swine on pig feed, rummaging in reeking sins.[24] What would you answer on that day, when you are supposed to give an account of your entire life, even of the least, useless words you once had uttered?[25]

Oh, you useless evil knave, you are well over ten thousand pounds in debt, and many a thousand times you have sinned against your GOD.[26] Oh, you unjust steward, how disgracefully you have brought down the gift of your mind, abusing your noble senses and your reasoning.[27] Cursed are you, for you did not heed what is written in the law of God.[28]

Oh, woe to me wretched human being, what have I done? Oh, what evil have I committed? Oh, wrath of the Most High, do not come upon me! Oh, fierceness of the Most High, who can bear you? Oh fright, oh terror, oh you scurrilous, sinful, reeking soul; I am enraged even with myself that I have become such an abhorrence before my God. Yes, my God! I am not worthy being called a human, treading on your land and soil. It should not come as a surprise if the earth opened up and devoured me, plunging me alive into hell.

Oh, repent and sigh, you wretched soul! oh, wail and weep, you wretched human being; if it were possible, you should indeed weep blood for your sins, and you should sigh with all your power. Oh, woe to you, you hardened heart, since no fright can soften you! woe to you, you sleeping heart, since no threat can awaken you. Oh, deadly sleep! since neither lightning nor thunder can deport you from God's grave law. Get up, dear soul, get up and rush toward penance, so that you will

---

[23] Matthew 7.

[24] Luke 15.

[25] Matthew 12:36-37.

[26] Matthew 18.

[27] Luke 16.

[28] Deuteronomy 27; Galatians 1.

not be seized in your sins. Behold, the day of the Lord is just outside the door, like a snare it will come upon you.[29] Behold, death will grasp at you, and in an instant he will get hold of you.

That is why I speak and why I am not silent; I confess and avow in front of my God everything that I have in my heart. Oh, if only I had enough water in my head, my eyes would be fountains of tears, so that I could weep about my sins day and night![30] Oh, weep, dear soul, let flow your tears day and night like a river, and do not stop, and let the tears from your eyes not subside because the Most High is angry about your sins.[31]

V.

Shall a person in such grief despair and in sin become dejected?

The second article of true penance.

Ah, this is God's aim: for now follows the second article of the Christian, true penance, which is the true and right faith in our Lord Jesus Christ, who has paid for our sins and reconciled us with God.[32] Here you shall recover again and learn to be comforted wholeheartedly by your dear Lord Christ – in this manner:

Oh, dearest Lord Jesus, you most pleasant savior! how very aggrieved my heart is to me. How frightened my soul is within my body. My God! you have crushed all my bones like a lion.[33] I pray to you that you may not disdain my frightened and stricken heart.[34] My Savior! reach out to me your hand of mercy, pull me up and do not let me

---

[29] Luke 21.
[30] Jeremiah 9:1a.
[31] Lamentations 2:18.
[32] Romans 5.
[33] Isaiah 38.
[34] Psalm 51.

drown in too much sadness.[35] Yes, my Lord, I thank you that you have stirred my heart, that you have let me recognize my sins, that you have granted me heartfelt remorse, since I have indeed been divinely saddened; but not to my detriment, FOR THE GODLY GRIEF BRINGS ABOUT A BLESSED REMORSE WHICH NO ONE REGRETS.[36]

Where, however, shall I seek comfort for my afflicted soul? Where shall I find peace and quiet for my stricken heart? Oh, with you, my dearest, most pleasant savior! with you alone, for you have come into this world to save poor sinners;[37] that is why you are named Jesus –which means, a helper and bliss-maker– so that you will save your people from all their sins.[38]

Here I am, my savior; while I am a great sinner, I am nevertheless a penitent sinner. Behold, I have heard your comforting voice when you called, COME TO ME ALL WHO ARE TROUBLED AND BURDENED, I WANT TO REFRESH YOU.[39] Lo and behold, my Lord! I come to you as well; yes I come and bring to you a much troubled, crushed, stricken, frightened heart.[40] Oh, refresh my wretched soul as well! Oh, heal my sinful conscience. Oh, you dear holy little lamb of God, who carries the world's sin[41] and takes it away, carry and take away from me all my guilt and sin, and forgive all my misdeeds.

You are indeed my savior, the sole sacrifice through which I am reconciled with God! FOR JUST AS MOSES HAS ELEVATED A SNAKE IN THE DESERT,[42] you have also been elevated on the cross, so that I and ALL WHO BELIEVE IN HIM SHALL NOT BE LOST, BUT INSTEAD HAVE ETERNAL LIFE.[43] I DO INDEED BELIEVE, MY GOD, BUT HELP ME OVERCOME MY

---

[35] 1st Corinthians 2.

[36] 2nd Corinthians 7:10a.

[37] 1st Timothy 2.

[38] Luke 2, Matthew 1.

[39] Matthew 11:28.

[40] Psalm 52; Isaiah 66.

[41] John 1.

[42] John 3:14a.

[43] John 3:14b.

WEAKNESS![44] Yes, Lord! you know all things.[45] You know that I believe
in you, even with a weak faith; nevertheless, with this weak faith of
mine I rely on you with all my trust and confidence. I believe and do
not doubt; I believe and trust that all my grievous and reeking sins
have certainly been atoned and paid for by your blood and death.

Yes, I know and I believe, I trust and I am certain, my Redeemer, that
your pure conception cleanses my sinful conception; that your immaculate birth sanctifies my impure birth; that your holy conduct
atones my sinful conduct; that your degradation is my elevation; that
your fright of hell is my comfort in heaven; that your bondage is my
salvation; that your ignominy is my honor; that your welts and bruises
are my adornment; that your execution is my initiation; that your suffering is my payment; that your merit is my ransom; that your lurid
death is the rightful guilt-offering for all my sin; that your obedience
is the just compensation for all my misdeeds; that your descent into
hell is my rescue from the forces of hell and of the devil; that your resurrection is my righteousness; and that your ascension to heaven is
my assurance that I am a certain heir of eternal life, and that through
you I have heaven already within me.[46]

Yes, my Lord Jesus, all this you have done for me, bestowed upon me,
and given to me;[47] and your heavenly Father takes this into my account, as assuredly as if I had earned all this myself and had carried
out the entire deed of redemption myself. Ah, be comforted, my soul,
and rejoice.[48] For you have the forgiveness of all your sins, you are just
before God, you have a merciful Father in heaven, you are an heir of
eternal life, and you have the token of your inheritance in your heart,
namely, the Holy Spirit, who awards witness to your spirit of being
God's child.[49] Who wants to accuse you now, dear soul? Here is
Christ, who has paid for us. Who wants to incriminate you, dear soul?

---

44 Mark 9:24.
45 John 21.
46 Romans 4.
47 Philippians 3.
48 Matthew 9.
49 Romans 8.

Here is God himself, who absolves and frees you, who declares you holy and just.

Do you still remember the harm that you have suffered through the original fall? Are you still upset about the perdition which overcame you through Adam? Oh, love and praise the name of the Lord, for you have received more in Christ Jesus, your Redeemer, than you have lost in Adam.[50] Oh, wonder of wonders, who can fathom that? Delight, my soul, and ponder this for a little; behold what you have lost and notice what you have gained.

1st. Behold how utterly the devil's attack has failed. For he intended to turn you away entirely from God your Lord, and to submerge you into God's eternal wrath and disgrace; but instead, Christ your LORD has not only reconciled the Father, appeased his wrath, and acquired eternal mercy, but he has also brought you to such indescribably high honors that you have become God's relative because he has himself assumed your very own flesh and blood.[51] You can indeed receive no greater honors unless you would become God himself.

2nd. Satan had intended to remove you from the pavilion in paradise, and thereby deprive you of the company of angels; but instead, Christ, your Savior, leads you not only into heavenly paradise and eternal life, but also raises you above all angels, making you sincere, for he has not taken on angelic, but human nature.[52]

3rd. Satan has intended to deprive you of the nourishment of life, and he has succeeded; for God the Lord cast out the humans for the sake of their sin, so that they shall not eat from the tree of life in paradise.[53] Christ, in contrast, has himself become your nourishment, and he is himself the tree of life,[54] which is much better than the other; for he spreads out his branches and arms so that

---

[50] Romans 5.

[51] Hebrews 1.

[52] Hebrews 2.

[53] Genesis 3.

[54] John 6.

we recline and move beneath him, eat of him, and become satisfied, so that we shall find tranquility and eternal peace under his shade.

4th. Satan had intended to deprive you of all your righteousness; he hurled you into sinning, robbed you of the inherited justice in which you had been made pure and without sin as an image of God. The Lord, in contrast, bestows on you a much better righteousness, namely, his merit and his fulfillment which is wholly credited to you through your faith, and which is your righteousness that applies in front of God alone.[55]

5th. Satan had intended to rob you of God's image through Adam's fall; he has marred all your strength; he has frayed you and left you dying[56] so that you were left without any strength of your own or without a single limb to do and fulfill God's will; thus, we would be forced to die and perish eternally. In contrast, however, Christ the Lord has not only has clothed you again with his own righteousness, has healed your wounds,[57] has redeemed you with his own blood and death, has let you be born again through his Holy Spirit, and has restored God's image; but he will also transfigure your wasted body at the day of judgment, and make it similar to his own transfigured body.[58]

6th. In summary, Satan had intended to deprive you of all your glory and hurl you into eternal damnation together with him. Christ, however, is ready to aid you; he not only accepts your flesh and blood, provides sufficiently for you, reconciles you with God, acquires forgiveness of sins, bestows upon you his righteousness, gives you the Holy Spirit and eternal life; but he also lifts you up to such great glory, that you have now become righteous before God, holy and free, a child of God, an heir of God, the Lord Christ's brother, his limb, his bride, his joint heir, a temple and a dwelling of the Holy Trinity, and an instrument of the Holy Spirit.

---

[55] Philippians 3.
[56] Luke 10.
[57] Isaiah 53.
[58] Philippians 3.

This means indeed, dear soul, *Omnia benè fecit*,[59] he has made every-thing well. Yes, my Lord! your name shall thus be praised in eternity. Oh, my God! how lovingly you comfort me, how eagerly you refresh my soul, how sweet your comfort is to me, how pleasantly my heart is contented.

You are indeed the righteous, golden portal of mercy toward eternal life; you are the way; you are the truth and the life; no one will come to the Father except through you.[60]

You are the way. FOR THERE IS IN NO OTHER SALVATION, NO OTHER NAME IS GIVEN TO HUMANS BY WHICH WE SHALL BECOME BLESSED.[61]

You are the truth. For whoever transgresses and does not stay within your teachings, he has no God. But he, who stays within your teach-ings, has both, you and your Father.

You are also the life. For whoever believes in you, he has eternal life. And he, who does not believe in you, will not see life, but the wrath of God remains over him.[62]

Oh, Lord Jesus! you are the only, eternal, rightful ladder toward heav-en[63] without which nobody can come to the Father,[64] grant me that I firmly hold on to you through true faith at all times, that I climb up to heaven through you, and that I inherit eternal life. Amen!

---

[59] Mark 7.
[60] John 14.
[61] Acts 4:12.
[62] John 3.
[63] Genesis 28.
[64] John 14.

VI.

Since I am now completely reconciled with God through Christ, made just before God through faith, and saved with hope even now, may I then behave as I wish until my dying hour arrives?

The third article of true penance.

 In truth, no! dear soul; if true faith is in your heart and you are newly born through the Holy Spirit, your mind will be inclined much differently. For newly born humans have a desire for new life.[65] And faith guards itself against reckless sinning, and it is loathsome and hostile toward all ungodly creatures. If a faithful human is assailed by Satan, and if he made a misstep from innate weakness,[66] he picks himself up again, regrets his fall daily, and finds comfort in his Lord Jesus; for this reason no condemnation is in him,[67] since he holds on to his Lord Christ Jesus through his faith.

And this is now the third article, which belongs to true Christian penance, namely, the new obedience according to God's ten commandments; therein, faith attests itself daily and shows itself in all good works toward God and humans, gratefully and lovingly. This you shall practice from now on daily:

I thank you, my God and heavenly Father, that you created me in your image.[68] And since I have fallen into sin and into your wrath,[69] you have bestowed upon me your dear son as a savior. How can I repay what you have done for me?[70] Govern me through your Holy Spirit, so that I yearn for your commandments; for human principles

---

[65] Romans 8.

[66] Proverbs 24.

[67] Romans 8.

[68] Genesis 1.

[69] Genesis 3.

[70] Psalm 116; Romans 5.

serve me to no purpose.[71] Grant me that I no longer live according to the flesh, but instead, according to the spirit;[72] and that I practice good virtues and have, at all times, faith and a good conscience.[73] Help me to become disposed like my Lord Jesus Christ, who has become my shining example, so that I follow his footsteps.[74] Strengthen me in your faith and hope so that I wrestle and fight to I resist Satan,[75] and that I do not follow the wicked world, for its course runs straight into hell.[76] Impart in me to crucify my sinful flesh daily and to lessen and defeat the desires of the flesh[77] so that my sins wither away from day to day, and that I apply myself to all chastity and virtue.[78] Help me to fear you, my Lord! at all times with all my heart, to love you with all my strength, and to keep all my desire and joy with you.[79] Grant me that I, your creature, rightly know you, my Creator! that I, contentedly and steadfastly, seek to honor your name, and that I call on you always in humility.[80] Convey to me always to carry desire and love for your word, and to be obedient in all your commandments.[81]

Lord Jesus Christ! ignite my heart with your love, so that I will always regard you as my highest treasure[82] and bear in mind how futile it is to be fond of this world. Turn my heart toward you, my savior, so that I deem the treasures of this world to be nothing and, instead, have yearning for the eternal goods.[83] Safeguard me from the wretched concern of food and drink, and help that I place no trust in the transitory.

---

[71] Matthew 15.

[72] Romans 8.

[73] 1st Timothy 1.

[74] 1st Peter 2.

[75] Ephesians 6.

[76] Romans 12; 1st John 2.

[77] Galatians 5.

[78] 1st Corinthians 9; Romans 9.

[79] Deuteronomy 6; Psalm 18.

[80] 1st Kings 10.

[81] Psalm 19; Ezekiel 20.

[82] Psalm 73.

[83] Matthew 6.

My Savior! grant me true patience in all suffering and tribulation, and impart steadfast courage and comfort in all contestation; help me, so that I do not despair in calamity, and that I be measured and restrained in fortune. Turn my heart toward godliness, and grant that I always do and bear in mind what you want, and that I serve you with a pure, sober, devout, chaste, righteous heart and with a willing mind.

My LORD! teach me always through your spirit and let me not fall in my weakness. Guide me with your right hand and stir in me to aim all my deeds and thoughts toward your good pleasure.

My God! help my heart not to be haughty, my disposition not to stray from you, my mouth to speak nothing wicked or abuse your name, to live soberly and measuredly, and not to overfill my body so as not to become unseemly.[84]

Grant me, my Lord! that I do not taunt my neighbor, nor defame him; that I do not abandon my vocation, that I do not seek wealth unjustly, that I do not strive for vain honor, that I neither be a hypocrite nor an idolater; grant me, my God! that I do not disdain the subordinates, that I reach out willingly to the needy, that I give gladly to the poor, that I do not aggrieve the miserable, that I be neither stingy nor jealous.

My Creator! take away from me all evil facetiousness, stubbornness, disquiet, impiety, heedlessness, idleness, laziness, negligence, ignorance, stubborn attitude, and unseemly behavior.

My God! my compassion! I beseech you by your dear son, give me an obedient heart at all times,[85] so that I become practiced in all works of love, and that I show kindheartedness toward all.

Help me to exchange good for evil at all times, to consign all revenge to God, to do good to my enemies, and to honor everyone. Help me to follow those who are godly and to avoid those who are wicked.

Grant me to assume virtuousness, and to flee all vices so that I may die as a declared enemy of all sin and shame.

---

[84] Romans 12, 13.
[85] 2nd Kings 3.

Let my heart remain with the only God, so that I fear your name,[86] and that I may examine and know myself as I walk on the righteous path and let my faith shine.

Redeem me in the end of all evil, and grant me to despise the earthly and seek the heavenly. Amen!

VII.

Is it sufficient if a person does rightful penance only for one time, or only once a year?

 Truly, no. For Christ the Lord teaches us to plead all day without ceasing, FORGIVE US OUR DEBT.[87] And Saint Peter says, GROW WITHIN THE GRACE AND THE COGNIZANCE OF OUR LORD JESUS CHRIST,[88] etc.

Even Saint Paul implores God the Lord on behalf of the Ephesians that they shall become strong from within through the Holy Spirit.[89] And David says, THEREFORE LET ALL THE FAITHFUL PRAY TO YOU WHILE YOU MAY BE FOUND.[90]

Do you hear this, dear soul, that you are not supposed to do penance for one time only, or once a year only, and then live again in heedless sin? Rather, your whole life shall and must be an everlasting penance. For if it is a Christian life, then it must also be a penitent life; for that is why you have been newly born through the Holy Baptism and have become a child of God, so that the old Adam in you –through daily remorse and penitence– will drown and die together with all sin and evil desires; and you shall then emerge again every day, resurrected as a new being who will live eternally, in piety and righteousness, before God.[91] Solomon speaks thus in Proverbs 4,

---

[86] Psalm 68.

[87] Matthew 6:12.

[88] 2 Peter 3:18.

[89] Ephesians 1.

[90] Psalm 32:6.

[91] Romans 6.

THE PATH OF THE RIGHTEOUS SHINES LIKE A LIGHT WHICH CAR-
RIES ON TO BE BRIGHT TILL THE FULL LIGHT OF DAY. [92]

Oh, God and Father of all mercy and kindheartedness! you have
called me in Christ Jesus to your eternal glory;[93] you granted me the
taste of the sweetness of your grace and cognizance, so that I have become a temple and dwelling of your Holy Spirit[94] and an heir of the
kingdom of heaven; govern me at all times through your Holy Spirit,
so that I always carry on in true penance, that I fight against all sin
without ceasing, that I build up cognizance of you, and that I grow in
all godliness as a newly born being; and, over time, that I become
stronger in faith. Grant me to rescue my soul, and not to look back,[95]
not to eat that which had been vomited like a dog,[96] and not to return
to wallowing in the mud like a swine,[97] and for my final condition not
to become worse than the first.[98] Indeed, my God! my strength ac-
complishes nothing, and soon I will be knocked down; you, however,
are the one who brings forth in me both, the intention and the completion[99] according to your good pleasure.[100] Ah, thereby you intend
to accomplish, to intensify, to strengthen, to establish, and to complete this work of yours which you have begun in me until my end.[101]

---

[92] Proverbs 4:18.
[93] 1st Peter 5.
[94] Romans 8.
[95] Genesis 19.
[96] Proverbs 26.
[97] 2nd Peter 2.
[98] Luke 11.
[99] Philippians 1.
[100] 1st Peter 5.
[101] Psalm 26

Do not let go of me, so that I do not let go of you; do not pull your hand away from me, God! my salvation. Explore me, my Lord! and come to know my heart; examine me to see what my intentions are, to find out whether I am on a wicked trail, and to lead me at all times on the everlasting, righteous path. Amen![102]

---

[102] Psalm 139:24

The 3rd Chapter.

Summarizes six distinguished articles
that belong to a Christian life
delightful to God.

I.
When I commence with daily penance, and when I
encounter much adversity on this narrow track,
how shall I behave so that my faith does
not end and that I do not go astray?

 That is indeed a necessary question, dear soul. For even as newly born beings who have become children of God through faith, we still carry these noble treasures in clay jars,[1] and in weak bodies; and when the devil is enraged with us, and when he tempts us with all his sorcery, then the world with its striking avenues harbors many wicked examples[2] that are utterly pleasing indeed to our tainted flesh and blood; and –with our eager feet leaping after it swiftly and merrily– we do not bear in mind that this wide trail leads straight into the abyss of hell. For this reason, dear soul, if you want to complete your life's course in a Christian manner, if you want to reach the end of faith, namely, the soul's salvation,[3] keep these six articles in mind daily –indeed, shelter them in your heart– so that you will abide by them throughout your lifetime.

1st. Firmly keep God's word and learn rightfully to understand, to share, and to use it.

2nd. Commemorate daily your Holy Baptism.

3rd. Partake often and diligently in Holy Communion.

---

[1] 2nd Corinthians 4.

[2] 1st John 2.

[3] 1st Peter 1.

4ᵗʰ. Learn to prepare rightfully for hardship and suffering.

5ᵗʰ. Stay within your vocation.

6ᵗʰ. Pray without ceasing.

Help, Lord Jesus Christ! help that I, an unwise and ignorant being, follow your word at all times, and that I abide by it my entire life, that I keep loyally the covenant of grace made with you at the Holy Baptism, that I partake often and worthily in your Holy Supper, that I bear the Holy Cross willingly, that I faithfully await my calling, and that I pray contentedly and wholeheartedly – so that I will spend the short time of my life in daily penance and in godliness, that I serve you and my neighbor well, and that I may remain steadfast in true faith until the end. Amen!

II.

Explain to me these six articles, so that I understand them well, and that I abide by them throughout my lifetime.

With great pleasure.

1ˢᵗ The word of God.
The first article belonging to a
Christian life.

 Firstly, I say,[4] FIRMLY KEEP GOD'S WORD AND ABIDE BY IT IN ALL YOUR INTENTIONS THROUGHOUT YOUR ENTIRE LIFE.[5] For thus speaks Scripture, YOUR WORD IS A LAMP FOR MY FEET AND A LIGHT ON MY PATH.[6] If you, dear soul, will now follow this light then you will walk along your life's course without blemish, and you will not fall. Learn, however, with all diligence to share the word of the Lord rightfully, and

---

[4] 1ˢᵗ Timothy 1.

[5] I Timothy 4:6.

[6] Psalm 119:105.

to keep well in mind the difference between the Law and the Gospels.[7]

I. God's Law –that is, the Ten Commandments–[8] is such a word and teaching wherein God commands and resolves that we shall conform to him within both, our heart and our entire life. That means that we shall love God, our Lord, with all our heart and with all our soul and with all our power; and that we love our neighbor as ourselves.[9] All this –which humans are capable neither of doing, nor of maintaining– you shall nevertheless contemplate daily in the Ten Commandments; and thereby, you shall learn to recognize your tainted nature and your sins,[10] and to follow a guideline by which to comply in your new conduct.[11]

II. The Gospel is such a word and teaching wherein God –out of pure grace and kindheartedness– offers and assures forgiveness of sins and eternal life to all who believe in Jesus Christ.[12] For all prophets bear witness of Jesus that –through his name– all who believe in him shall receive forgiveness of sins.[13] Therefore, you must not lose sight of this sermon of grace, so that your heart will be comforted when assailed by sin and all temptations of the devil, and that you can joyously surrender to God in all afflictions, even in death.

Keep well in mind, dear soul, that both teachings are God's word;[14] both have been commanded since the beginning of the church of God; both must also endure and neither be dismissed. For this reason learn to regard both teachings in great judiciousness; nevertheless, distinguish them rightfully and apply each at the right time.

---

[7] 2nd Timothy 2.

[8] Exodus 20.

[9] Matthew 22; Deuteronomy 6; Leviticus 19.

[10] Romans 3.

[11] Ezekiel 20.

[12] John 3.

[13] Acts 10.

[14] Luke 10.

1st. As you, dear soul, contemplate daily the Ten Commandments, and as you thereby recognize your utter failure in conforming to the will of God, you will also see that –since all your powers have perished through Adam's fall– you cannot keep any of God's commandments, and that you have thereby earned the wrath of God and eternal damnation for your sins. However, do not despair, but thank God for his commandments and for bringing you to recognize your sins. Next to knowing Jesus Christ, nothing can be of more benefit to you than recognizing your sins; for Christ and his good deeds are unbecoming to a human unless he recognizes his sins before he faces the wrath of God.

2nd. When Satan comes, making the sin too great for you, and when he threatens you with the fiery wrath of God, with hell and eternal damnation, then find comfort in the holy gospel's sermon of grace, and be restored with the following or with other comforting verses from the gospels: FOR GOD HAS LOVED THE WORLD THAT HE GAVE HIS ONE AND ONLY SON, THAT ALL WHO BELIEVE IN HIM SHALL NOT PERISH BUT HAVE ETERNAL LIFE.[15] Also, AS SURE AS I LIVE, I TAKE NO PLEASURE IN THE DEATH OF A POOR SINNER, BUT RATHER THAT HE TURNS AROUND AND LIVES.[16] Also, I WILL DELIVER THIS PEOPLE FROM THE POWER OF THE GRAVE; I WILL REDEEM THEM FROM DEATH.[17] Also, WHERE SIN INCREASED, GRACE INCREASED ALL THE MORE.[18] Also, THIS IS CERTAINLY TRUE AND A MOST WORTHY SAYING, THAT JESUS CHRIST CAME INTO THIS WORLD TO SAVE THE SINNERS.[19] THEREFORE, RESIST SATAN FIRMLY IN FAITH,[20] so that he will depart from you. Of these sayings of comfort you are assured, and

---

[15] John 3:16.
[16] Ezekiel 33:11.
[17] Hosea 13:14.
[18] Romans 5:20.
[19] 1st Timothy 1:15.
[20] 1st Peter 5:9.

their avowal for you stands much firmer even than heaven and earth. For his word is the truth.[21]

3rd. When Satan, however, approaches from another flank, when he disguises himself as an angel of light,[22] when he makes sin appear small and the wrath of God meager, and when he whispers in your ear that sin can easily be atoned because grace is sufficiently at hand: watch out, dear soul; do not give in; keep in mind again the severe law of God wherein all sins are being charged so dreadfully; that is why sin can be neither meager, nor small. Keep also in mind the fright of your dear Lord Jesus Christ, and speak within your heart: fie! you, Satan, you liar! I see how hard and egregious it became for my Lord Jesus, who has once atoned me for my sins under the curse of the law, and who has borne his Father's wrath for me; that is why I want to hate each and every sin throughout my entire life; and I want to guard against sin as I guard against the devil himself. I thank my God that he once redeemed me from sins and from the devil's harnesses. Should I entangle myself yet again in his tethers? THE TETHERS ARE ASUNDER, AND I AM FREE; MAY THE LORD'S NAME STAND BY ME, THE CREATOR OF HEAVEN AND EARTH.[23]

4th. When Satan, however, shows you the beautiful course of the world, and when he tempts you to its desires, then keep in mind the solemn laws of God, and contemplate St. Paul's words when he says, DO NOT CONFORM TO THIS WORLD, BUT RATHER CHANGE YOURSELVES THROUGH RENEWING YOUR MIND.[24] Oh, watch out, dear soul, you know your flesh and blood well; how utterly drawn it is toward worldly matters; instead, force yourself to follow the solemn voice of the law, for the world's path runs straight into hell.

---

[21] Luke 21; John 17.

[22] 2nd Corinthians 11.

[23] Psalm 124.

[24] Romans 12:2.

5th. When he mocks you for being poor and for suffering from hunger and depravity, then recite scripture of the gospels, MAN LIVES NOT ON BREAD ALONE, BUT ON EVERY WORD THAT COMES FROM THE MOUTH OF GOD.[25] And also, YOU, LORD! MAKE JOYFUL MY HEART, EVEN IF THEIR WINE AND GRAIN ABOUND.[26] These words do not deceive. For thus says the Lord, MY TRUTH I SHALL NOT LET FAIL.[27]

6th. When he points out that you are wretched, sick, abandoned, then resist him and say, I MAY WELL BE POOR AND WRETCHED, BUT THE LORD PROVIDES FOR ME.[28] For this reason, if I have only you, my God! if I have only you, then I ask for nothing more in heaven and on earth. AND EVEN IF MY BODY AND SOUL WASTE AWAY, YOU ARE STILL MY HEART'S COMFORT AND PART OF ME.[29] On this, my soul, depend for your entire life. For thus says the Lord, I WILL NOT ALTER WHAT CAME FROM MY MOUTH.[30] And also, I HAVE MADE A COVENANT, AND I WILL NOT LIE.[31]

7th. When he frightens you with death, resist him with a faithful heart and say, thus speaks the Lord, YOUR DEAD WILL LIVE, AND THEIR BODIES WILL RISE.[32] To this end I believe in a merciful forgiveness of all my sins, in a resurrection of the flesh, and in an eternal life. All this is certainly true for me, and I rely completely on it. For heaven and earth will fade away, but God's word will not; it will remain and last into eternity.[33] And all, who keep to the word, and who wrap themselves into the word, shall be sustained eternally together with the word and within the word.

---

[25] Matthew 4:4.

[26] Psalm 4:7.

[27] Psalm 89:33.

[28] Psalm 40:17.

[29] Psalm 73:26a.

[30] Psalm 89:34b.

[31] Psalm 89:35.

[32] Isaiah 26:19.

[33] Luke 21, Isaiah 40.

Lord Jesus Christ! you, the king of eternal truth! help that I always keep in mind your true, holy word, your law and gospel to guide all my thoughts and deeds. Teach me through your Holy Spirit to understand your word rightfully, to discern it rightfully,[34] and to apply it at the right time. Grant that I keep your laws in mind daily, so that I do not forget my sin and my insignificance. Write your verses of comfort also into my heart and remind me of them in all my concerns, so that they become my guards and weapons to defeat my enemy, my armor and shield[35] against the devil, my rod and staff[36] holding and guiding me, my nourishment and refreshment in all fright and affliction. Grant me to cloak and wrap myself completely in your word, to rise with it and go to sleep with it; indeed, to live according to your word, to die according to your word, and to arise again according to your word. And when my weak heart would lose hope, then help me not to despair, for your word does not betray me. I know and I believe, GOD, the eternal truth! that you will keep your word: and that is why I will be sustained indeed. I know and I believe that you do not lie; therefore, I cannot be betrayed. And when my heart wavers and becomes disparaged, your word and assurance do not waver; you are greater and your word is more assured to me than even my own heart.[37] That is why I do not let myself be dismayed. Amen!

2nd Baptism.
The second article belonging to a
Christian life.

Secondly, dear soul, you shall remind and comfort yourself daily of your Holy Baptism, wherein the Lord your God has cleansed you and accepted you as his child,[38] and wherein he has entered a covenant of grace with you that he shall be your merciful God and Father, and that

---

[34] 2nd Timothy 2.
[35] Proverbs 30.
[36] Psalm 23.
[37] 1st John 3.
[38] 1st Peter 3.

you shall be his dear child and heir. Indeed, my soul, at the Holy Baptism your Lord Jesus has called you by your name before you even knew him; yes, he has given you a name, and, according to his name, he has called you a Christian[39] – an irrevocable testimony that you are Jesus' brother and joint heir,[40] and that you shall have everything which he has purchased and acquired, namely, forgiveness of sins, righteousness, the Holy Spirit, and eternal life.

Therefore, dear soul, as often as you speak the articles of faith, I BELIEVE IN GOD THE FATHER, etc., I BELIEVE IN JESUS CHRIST HIS ONE AND ONLY SON, etc., I BELIEVE IN GOD THE HOLY SPIRIT, etc., find comfort in the certainty of belonging to the number of those of whom the Lord says, WHOEVER BELIEVES AND IS BAPTIZED WILL BE SAVED.[41] However, do withdraw from all ungodly people of whom the Lord says, WHOEVER DOES NOT BELIEVE WILL BE CONDEMNED.[42] Indeed, such cognizance reminds you that through baptism you are bound to the same covenant, that you shall not live according to the will and desire of your flesh,[43] but that you shall serve the living God in piety and righteousness pleasing to him.[44]

I thank you, my Lord Jesus Christ! for your indescribable kindness: not only that you have pulled me alive from the womb, but also –since I was deceased in sins– that you have let me come to the Holy Baptism and thereby included me in your covenant of mercy.[45] Through your spirit you let me be newly born, you tore me away from the devil's vengeance, and you accepted me as your child and heir of heaven before I even knew you. My Savior! how can I repay you for what you

---

[39] Isaiah 45 and 62; Jeremiah 14.

[40] Romans 8.

[41] Mark 16:16a.

[42] Mark 16:16b.

[43] Romans 8.

[44] Luke 1.

[45] 1ˢᵗ Peter 3.

have done for me?[46] I beseech you, govern and sustain me though your Holy Spirit, to stand firm daily in the covenant of mercy,[47] to find heartfelt comfort therein, to keep my faith safe, to cling to you, my God, to discard all idolatry, superstition, and sorcery, and at all times to serve your name intimately in spirit and joyously in hope.[48]

Yes, my God! because I have departed from sin through baptism, and because I have become a new being,[49] grant me therefore and help me also from now on to walk within a new life, so that my life will give witness, both to God and to humans, of having received the Holy Baptism – beneficially and blessedly. Guide and lead me wholly through this arduous vale of tears, and never leave me until you will bring me into the kingdom of eternal salvation where you will grant me all treasures and goods of mercy which you have promised, presented, and pledged to me at my Holy Baptism.

3rd The Lord's Supper.
The third article belonging to a
Christian life

 Thirdly, dear soul, do attend diligently at all times the Holy Communion of the Lord.[50] For here is the table which the Lord has prepared for his new-born children; here is the food with which he refreshes and strengthens the baptized new human beings. For thus speaks the Lord, your savior,[51] TAKE THIS AND EAT; THIS IS MY BODY, WHICH WILL BE GIVEN FOR YOU FOR THE FORGIVENESS OF SINS. And also, TAKE THIS AND DRINK FROM IT ALL OF YOU; THIS CUP IS THE NEW TESTAMENT IN MY BLOOD, WHICH WILL BE POURED OUT FOR YOU FOR THE FORGIVENESS OF SINS.

---

[46] Psalm 116.
[47] 1st Peter 3.
[48] Ephesians 1.
[49] Romans 6.
[50] 1st Corinthians 11.
[51] Matthew 26; Mark 14; Luke 22; 1st Corinthians 11.

Do you hear, my soul, what the Lord, your Savior, has prepared for you at his table? Truly, not only bread and wine, but also his holy body and his holy blood. For the bread which we break is indeed the communion of the body of Christ; and the consecrated cup which we bless is indeed the communion of the blood of Christ.[52]

That is why I believe and know that my Lord Jesus Christ, God and human being, is himself present at this beneficence; and with bread and wine he gives me his true body to eat and his true blood to drink, according to his pledge and command. Indeed, my Lord Jesus! you are yourself the host, and I am your guest: behold, here I come –a wretched person– I come out of the desert of this dire world, full of exertion and sorrow; and I bring to you a hungry, frail, thirsty, and yet a faithful heart. My Lord Jesus! restore me at your table, and strengthen me with your food, so that I will become satisfied and blessed.

Come near, my soul, and rush to your Lord's Supper, so that your faith will be strengthened, and your heart will be restored. Oh, do not disbelieve any longer, but believe.[53] For behold, here the Lord, your Redeemer, assures you through a certain sign, a pledge, a seal that you, out of sheer grace and kindheartedness, shall be an irrefutable heir of his goods; and he bestows everything unto you which he has acquired with the sacrifice of his body and blood; namely, forgiveness of all your sins, righteousness which applies before God, and eternal life.[54] All this shall certainly belong to you as if you had hung on the cross and you had acquired all this yourself: indeed, he thereby bears witness to you that you are deemed –for his sake before God– to be just, pure, holy, and indeed, dear, pleasing, and sacred as your Lord Christ himself.

And furthermore, in doing this he lowers himself through his Holy Spirit into your faithful heart and soul, and he wants to accompany you with eternal, living comfort, never to leave

---

[52] 1st Corinthians 11.

[53] John 20.

[54] Genesis 15; Romans 4.

you again and to bring forth a new life, light and joy within you. Yes, my Lord Jesus! thus am I within you, and you within me.[55] I cling to you, my Redeemer! I cling to you as firmly as a living limb to its living body,[56] as a bride to her bridegroom, being flesh of your flesh and bone of your bone. Indeed, I am within you, and I cling to you like the grapes to its vine and a branch to its root;[57] and thus I obtain from you and through you always new sustenance and strength, new comfort and joy, new life and refreshment; and in this manner I am united with you in body and soul through true faith; and I am united through the Holy Spirit so that neither affliction nor death shall separate me from you forever.[58]

Praise be to you, Lord, my Savior, that you have cared for me in such a fatherly manner, and that you have arranged for me this supper of mercy, from which I may get food and sustenance for my hungry heart and comfort and refreshment for my thirsty soul, so that I carry on in faith firmly and strongly, that I follow you contentedly, my Redeemer! that I remain firmly with you, and that I may steadfastly endure until the end. Amen!

You have also said, my Lord Jesus! DO THIS IN MY REMEMBRANCE.[59] My God, what delightful remembrance this is to me; how it comforts my yearning soul! Indeed, my Lord Jesus! when I eat and drink at your table, then I embrace both, your name's remembrance of comfort and your name's remembrance of thanksgiving.

1st. Firstly, I will keep the remembrance of comfort by observing all holidays throughout the year in my heart, by contemplating all your good deeds, by internalizing them, and by finding comfort in them.

2nd. At your table I will observe a merry Christmas. For your Holy Supper witnesses to me that you have indeed taken on my flesh and

---

[55] John 15.

[56] Ephesians 5.

[57] John 15.

[58] Romans 8.

[59] Matthew 26; Mark 14; Luke 22; 1st Corinthians 11.

blood; and that you have befriended me much more dearly than your holy angels, for you did not assume angelic but human nature.

3ʳᵈ. At your table I also observe the endearing Week of Passion. For your Holy Supper attests to me that you have become the equitable guilt-offering for my sin. Indeed, here I eat the rightful Passover lamb;[60] namely, you, Lord Jesus! who has been sacrificed and slain for me.

4ᵗʰ. At your table I will also observe a happy Easter. Since I am part of your body and blood and I am your limb, I believe and hope–just like you have arisen from the dead and have lived–[61] that I will also not remain in the grave as a limb, but that I shall rise again, live, and reign.

5ᵗʰ. At your table I will also observe a happy day of Ascension. For, since you have borne witness in the communion that I am within you and you are within me, and that I am a limb of your body, so too will I once ascend to heaven with my body and live there eternally, where you live, my Lord and my entire being![62]

6ᵗʰ. At your table I will observe a happy Pentecost. For your Holy Supper bears witness to me that you live in my heart, and that through your Holy Spirit I unite and connect with you; and thereby you seal my salvation so that your Spirit will stay with me at all times as a pledge of my eternal inheritance;[63] that it will awaken life and comfort in me, that it will ignite peace and joy, and that it will bear witness of my spirit of being your brother and eternal joint heir.[64]

7ᵗʰ. At your table I will also observe the feast of the Holy Trinity, and I find comfort that from now on I shall be a temple of God for all times, and that the entire Holy Trinity will come to me and will dwell inside

---

[60] 1ˢᵗ Corinthians 5.
[61] 1ˢᵗ Corinthians 15.
[62] 1ˢᵗ Corinthians 15.
[63] Ephesians 1.
[64] Romans 8.

me;[65] indeed, that I will also own eternal salvation after this life, and that I will see the Lord my GOD face to face.

8th. At your table I will also observe the rightful All Saints Day; and I find comfort in the blissful harmony and community which I and your dear saints have with you through true faith, Lord Jesus! and through you also with the Father and the Holy Spirit, as you have promised: WHOEVER EATS MY FLESH AND DRINKS MY BLOOD STAYS WITHIN ME AND I WITHIN HIM.[66] And also, THAT YOU ALSO BECOME ONE; JUST LIKE YOU, FATHER! BECOME ONE WITHIN ME, AND I WITHIN YOU, THAT THEY ALSO BECOME ONE IN US.[67] Indeed, my Lord! SINCE IT IS ONE BREAD, MANY OF US ARE ONE BODY SINCE WE ALL HAVE BECOME PART OF ONE BREAD.[68] Oh, my Lord! how my soul rejoices about such heavenly company, and how happy I become at your table; and I know for certain that I, together with all saints, will inherit and own all your treasures and goods eternally.

9th. Indeed, my Lord Jesus! so says also your holy apostle, AS OFTEN AS YOU EAT OF THIS BREAD AND DRINK OF THIS CUP, YOU SHALL PRONOUNCE THE LORD'S DEATH UNTIL HE ARRIVES.[69] That is why I will also observe the Feast of the Holy Future[70] at your table; and I look forward to your appearance when you will visibly return to complete this supper together with all sermons, and when you will take me to you, so that I will be where you are,[71] where you have prepared another eternal, heavenly meal in your Father's kingdom, where I will sit at the table with Abraham, Isaac, Jacob, and with all your saints, and where I will eat the bread of life eternally.[72] Oh, how yearningly I contemplate this table of yours and sigh from the bottom of my heart:

---

[65] John 14.

[66] John 6:56.

[67] John 17:21a.

[68] 1st Corinthians 10:17.

[69] 1st Corinthians 11:22.

[70] Possibly the 2nd Sunday of Advent.

[71] John 17.

[72] Matthew 8.

Lord Jesus, come; indeed, come soon, my Savior! and do not delay. Amen![73]

10th. Furthermore, my God! at your table I will also observe the rightful Thanksgiving of your name. Since you have fed me so abundantly, my heart glows with rightful thankfulness toward you. And I thank you for each and every one of your kindnesses which you have bestowed on me –a poor sinner– on my body and on my soul for all my life.

Indeed, I observe your great feasts and thank you heartily for your creation, for your revelation, for you becoming human, for your redemption, for your holy word, for the faith which you have given me, for your Holy Spirit which you have poured into my heart, for your most worthy sacraments, and for all bodily and spiritual gifts and goods. My God! how can I fathom everything? How can I, in my weakness, article all the great things you have done for my soul?[74]

Help me, Lord Jesus, my Savior! to be present at your table, frequently and often, and to observe your remembrances with joy. Behold, I am your brother and your joint heir: my God! I am your child, and I belong to your kingdom; where else shall I go than to your table? Help me, Lord, my Redeemer! to observe your holy festive days devoutly and without ceasing, to strengthen my heart and faith so that all my desire and highest joy is with you, to thank you heartily for your great kindnesses, to serve you with all my heart until my end, and–after this vale of tears– to eat the bread of life in your kingdom together with all the chosen. Amen!

Finally, dear soul, whenever you eat the bread of the Lord and drink from his cup, do not forget about your neighbor who is also partaking next to you.

Indeed, my Lord Jesus, I avow that my neighbor also is a limb, your brother, a child of God, and your joint heir, just as I am; that is why I am wholeheartedly fond of him for your sake, and I am ready to treat him in all kindheartedness as I treat myself.

---

[73] Revelation 22.

[74] Luke 1.

And when you bless my little fountain, and when you multiply my nourishment, then I will have the poor enjoy it as well; for you feed me with your bread, and you give me to drink from your cup; shall I thus not also feed my brother –your joint heir– with my bread, and shall I not restore him with what you have provided for me? Govern me, my Lord Jesus! with your Holy Spirit, that I wholeheartedly love my neighbor at all times; and that I sincerely tend to the afflicted, feed the hungry, give the thirsty to drink, willingly give shelter to the stranger, clothe the naked, comfort the sick, and readily serve all the poor and the ones in need.[75] Help me to keep in mind at all times the great word which will come from your mouth on that day. TRULY, I SAY TO YOU, WHAT YOU HAVE DONE TO ONE OF THESE, MY MOST MISERABLE BROTHERS, THAT YOU HAVE DONE TO ME.[76] And also, TRULY, I SAY TO YOU, WHAT YOU HAVE NOT DONE TO ONE OF THESE OF THE MOST MISERABLE, THAT YOU HAVE ALSO NOT DONE TO ME.[77] Amen.

4th The daily cross and suffering of the children of God.
The fourth article belonging to a Christian life.

 Fourthly, my soul, learn to ready yourself well for the daily cross of suffering which the children of God will always have to bear for their Lord in this vale of sorrows. Thus speaks the Holy Spirit, WE MUST ENTER THE KINGDOM OF GOD THROUGH MUCH TRIBULATION.[78]

Indeed, my soul, the teaching of the cross belongs to the greatest mysteries which the human mind cannot readily comprehend; this mystery, like others, is revealed only in God's word, and it must be learned from there. That is why, dear soul, the cross has become such a burden for us, and we are frightened about God abandoning us altogether or becoming

---

75 Isaiah 58; Matthew 25.

76 Matthew 25:40b.

77 Matthew 25:40b.

78 Acts 14:22b.

our worst enemy. This is fittingly revealed by the two dear disciples who went from Jerusalem to Emmaus in grief and sorrow and to whom the Lord appeared in another guise; their eyes, however, were restrained so that they did not recognize him.[79] Behold, my soul, this is the appearance of the cross which the Lord often puts on to conceal himself, appearing as a stranger even to his dearest children.[80] This, however, is his delight and pleasure for the faithful on his earth.[81] Indeed, at times he will treat them so harshly that they may think God had forgotten love and kindness, but in time he will make himself familiar again and fill their hearts with joy. Therefore, dear soul, learn to ready yourself well for this mystery, and keep well in mind the following seven rules of the cross; then your tribulations will become not even half as burdensome.

The 1ˢᵗ rule of the cross.

1ˢᵗ. All the faithful are commanded by God to become Christ's cross-bearers. Thus says Saint Paul, FOR WHOM GOD HAD PREVIOUSLY CHOSEN, HE ALSO PREDESTINED TO BE CONFORMED TO THE IMAGE OF HIS SON, THAT HE MIGHT BE THE FIRSTBORN AMONG MANY BROTHERS.[82] Have you taken notice, my soul, that you have been commanded to bear the cross of suffering, not only in the womb, but even before the world was formed, so that you shall become like and akin to your Lord Jesus! Indeed, my soul, you are flesh of his flesh and bone of his bone; why would you not suffer with him? He is the Lord, and you are his disciple; he is the bridegroom, and you are his bride; he is the head, and you are his limbs.[83] Why would you want to be better off than he? Look at the Lord, the chief of the cross, and behold how all dear saints have followed him in

---

[79] Luke 24.

[80] Proverbs 8.

[81] Isaiah 64.

[82] Romans 8:29.

[83] Luke 2, Ephesians 4.

tribulation.[84] The Lord leads with the largest cross and the faithful follow, all carrying their burden with the joyous hope they will become akin to him in eternal glory[85] after trying to be like the Lord Jesus here in tribulation.[86]

Oh, Lord, my God! you have commanded and prepared me to be the cross bearer of your son; grant me an understanding heart to recognize such wonderful council and to accept the cross with joy so that I will follow my savior and become akin to him – here temporally, and there eternally. Amen!

The 2nd rule of the cross.

2nd. It is the Lord Christ's command that his faithful shall carry his cross after him. For this he says, TAKE MY YOKE UPON YOU.[87] And also, WHOEVER WANTS TO FOLLOW ME MUST DENY HIMSELF, AND TAKE UP HIS CROSS DAILY AND FOLLOW ME.[88] Indeed, my soul, this command does not concern the nonbelievers, but his saints and his faithful. For the cross of the Lord is a precious gem, and the Lord will not entrust it to nonbelievers. Indeed, he will not grant such an adornment to any of the ungodly. Look at Simon from Cyrene, what an honor it was for him to carry the cross behind the Lord;[89] what fame he will attain on the day of the last judgment!

Oh, my Lord Jesus; you, who has commanded me to bear your cross; grant me also an obedient heart to take on your yoke joyously and to follow you willingly in all suffering. Amen![90]

---

[84] Matthew 24.

[85] 1st Corinthians 5.

[86] Romans 8.

[87] Matthew 11:29a.

[88] Luke 9:23.

[89] Luke 23.

[90] Luke 9; 1st Kings 3.

The 3ʳᵈ rule of the cross.

3ʳᵈ. The Lord Christ has three schools of the cross: firstly, a school of chastisement in which he punishes his own for the sake of their sin; secondly, a school of trial in which he tries their faith, hope, and prayer; thirdly, a school of torment in which he lets his own be persecuted and killed in his name.[91] Take notice, my soul, for you are also a disciple and student of your Lord, and he will most certainly also lead you into one of his schools every day. When he punishes you for your sins, like dear David, so thank him for his chastising and say, IT IS GOOD FOR ME THAT YOU HAVE CHASTISED ME, SO THAT I WILL LEARN YOUR RULES.[92] When he tries you and when he directs you unexpectedly,[93] like dear Joseph and Job, so keep in mind that he tries your faith, he awakens your hope, and he urges your prayer.[94] When he honors you by suffering persecution or death for his sake, then be wholeheartedly pleased of your worthiness of suffering ignominy in his name.[95]

Lord Jesus Christ! you were not ashamed to hang on the cross in scorn and shame; grant me also not to be ashamed of standing with the virgin Mary under the cross.[96] If you can lead me wondrously, then help me to follow you wondrously and be ready to give my life for your sake whenever it pleases you. Amen!

The 4ᵗʰ rule of the cross.

4ᵗʰ. The suffering of the faithful is a sign of God's love and not of his wrath. For this says the Lord, WHOEVER I LOVE, THOSE I PUNISH AND CHASTISE.[97] And also, THE WORLD WILL RE-

---

[91] 1ˢᵗ Corinthians 11; Psalm 119; Isaiah 28; ibid 26; Psalm 44; Romans 8.

[92] Psalm 119:71.

[93] Psalm 4.

[94] Isaiah 26.

[95] Acts 5.

[96] John 19.

[97] Revelation 3:19.

JOICE, BUT YOU WILL BE SAD.[98] Likewise, THE JUDGMENT BEGINS IN THE HOUSE OF GOD.[99] And also, THE CITY THAT IS NAMED AFTER ME, I WILL BEGIN TO HARASS.[100] Do you hear that, my soul? Indeed, dear soul, whoever loves his child will discipline it.[101] For where is a father who does not chastise his son? If you, however, are without chastisement –which all children of God have tasted– then you are a bastard and not a child. Look at your Lord Jesus, the one and only child of God; how strict was his father with him? How severely was he beaten for the sake of the sins of others?[102]

Help, Lord Jesus! that I do not get scared of your chastising rod, but that I kiss it like a pious child, and that I thank you at all times for your chastisement. Amen![103]

The 5th rule of the cross.

5th. The greater the affliction, the nearer God is. For this says the Lord, I AM WITH HIM IN AFFLICTION; I WILL TEAR HIM FREE, AND HONOR HIM.[104] Oh, my soul, how utterly flesh and blood will not believe that. When in tribulation, we always think that God has exposed us to the devil and to all misfortune. No, my soul, even though Satan is your worst enemy, scheming day and night to bring misfortune upon you, he cannot harm a hair of yours without the Lord's will.[105] Yes, dear soul, how can God forget us? How can he lie who himself is the truth?[106] And even if he conceals himself for a brief moment, he will bring us back

---

[98] John 16:20b.
[99] 1st Peter 4:17a.
[100] Jeremiah 25:29a.
[101] Hebrew 12.
[102] Isaiah 53.
[103] Psalm 116.
[104] Psalm 91:15b.
[105] Matthew 10.
[106] Isaiah 10.

again in great compassion.[107] FOR THE PIOUS, THE LIGHT DAWNS EVEN IN DARKNESS FROM A GRACIOUS AND COMPASSIONATE GOD.[108] IF GOD IS WITH ME, WHO WILL BE AGAINST ME?[109] What can I lose when I still have my God?

Lord Jesus! if only I have you, then I do not ask for anything in heaven and on earth; indeed, EVEN IF MY BODY AND SOUL WASTES AWAY, YOU ARE ALWAYS, LORD! MY HEART'S COMFORT AND MY PORTION.[110] Amen!

The 6ᵗʰ rule of the cross.

6ᵗʰ. The suffering of God's children always serves for the best of them and never for the worst. For this says Saint Paul, WE KNOW THAT TO THOSE WHO LOVE GOD ALL THINGS SERVE FOR THE GOOD.[111] And also, WOUNDS FROM A FRIEND CAN BE TRUSTED.[112] Yes, my soul, suffering serves for the good in many ways.

For sin teaches us to know what is written, I WILL CHASTISE YOU WITH MEASURE,[113] so that you do not think of yourself as innocent.

Suffering also compels us to the word. For contestation alone teaches us to take notice of the word.[114]

Suffering awakens our faith, as it is written, and such tribulation has come about us, so that we do not place confidence in ourselves, but in God who resurrects the dead.[115]

---

[107] Isaiah 54.

[108] Psalm 112:4.

[109] Romans 8:31.

[110] Psalm 73:26.

[111] Romans 8:28a.

[112] Proverbs 27:6.

[113] Jeremiah 30:11.

[114] Isaiah 28.

[115] 1ˢᵗ Corinthians 1.

Suffering also teaches us rightful prayer. For it is written, LORD! WHEN IN DISTRESS, THEN THEY LOOK FOR YOU; AND WHEN YOU CHASTISE THEM, THEN THEY CRY OUT FRIGHTENED.[116]

Suffering teaches us to avoid sin, as it is written, MAKE CERTAIN, SINCE YOU HAVE BECOME HEALTHY, NOT TO SIN FROM NOW ON, SO THAT NOTHING WORSE WILL HAPPEN TO YOU.[117]

Suffering makes us weary of this life and awakens in us a desire for the eternal, as it is written, FOR HERE WE DO NOT HAVE AN ENDURING CITY, BUT WE ARE LOOKING FOR THE CITY THAT IS TO COME.[118]

Yes, my soul, to the faithful everything must wholly serve for the good, as Saint Augustine writes, EVEN SIN ITSELF WORKS FOR THEIR GOOD.[119] We have, indeed, gained more through Christianity than we have lost through sin.

Lord Jesus Christ! write this pleasing comfort into my heart, and safeguard me from despairing in any tribulation, but help me to commend myself to you eternally, assured –even in the death– of the very best; for wondrous is your word which leads everything to glory. Amen![120]

The 7ᵗʰ rule of the cross.

7ᵗʰ. Patience, prayer, and hope will not let any suffering become too unbearable. For this says the prophet Jeremiah, IT IS A DELIGHTFUL THING TO BE PATIENT, AND TO HOPE FOR THE HELP OF THE LORD.[121] And David says, CALL ON ME IN AFFLICTION, SO WILL I RESCUE YOU, AND YOU WILL PRAISE ME.[122] And Sirach says, LOOK AT THE GENERATIONS OF OLD, AND KEEP THEM IN MIND: HAS ANY EVER BEEN PUT TO SHAME, WHO HAS TRUSTED IN

---

[116] Isaiah 26:16.

[117] John 5:14b.

[118] Hebrews 13:14.

[119] Soliloquies of Augustine: Book I, chapter 28.

[120] Isaiah 28.

[121] Lamentations 3:26.

[122] Psalms 50:15.

GOD?[123] Yes, my soul, when someone carries a burden or a load and seizes it rightfully, to him it will not become half as heavy, particularly when he has help and relief. That is why patience, prayer, hope are like hands or arms for the faithful heart to seize its tribulations and to carry on more agreeably. For patience does everything contentedly; therefore, nothing becomes too difficult. Prayer comes through to GOD, and it will certainly attain either rescue or relief. And hope does not put us to shame,[124] but it knows for certain that God is loyal, and it prevents temptation that is too excessive or too severe.[125] Impatience, however, angers God; it deters prayer and makes everything difficult.

Take as an example your Lord Jesus, and learn all this from him.[126] Look also at dear Job, and learn as well to say in your affliction, EVEN IF THE LORD WOULD RATHER KILL ME, I WILL NEVERTHELESS PLACE MY HOPE IN HIM.[127]

Lord Jesus Christ! give me always a patient heart, one that can wait and pray well, so that in my suffering I do not become impatient, but comforted, that I will confidently toss all my concerns at you, and that I may always hope for the best from you. Amen![128]

5ᵗʰ A Christian's outward vocation.
The fifth article belonging to a
Christian life.

 Fifthly, dear soul, remain within your vocation, wherein you have been placed by God, and stay there with all diligence and loyalty, so that you can account for all

---

[123] Sirach 2:10.

[124] Romans 5.

[125] 2ⁿᵈ Corinthians 10.

[126] 1ˢᵗ Peter 2.

[127] Job 13:15a.

[128] Sirach 2.

your deeds in front of God and humans.[129] For God the Lord does not want humans to be idle, but rather for each human to be issued labor according to his measure.[130] God the Lord himself is indeed not idle, but he works, governs, bears, and arranges all things; he protects, blesses, grants, and rescues all pious hearts, as Christ says himself, MY FATHER HAS BEEN WORKING UNTIL NOW, AND I TOO AM WORKING.[131] Yes, my soul, should God the Lord be idle for just one moment, the whole world would go under.

Likewise, the holy angels are ghosts, always ready for service, sent to serve those who shall inherit salvation.[132] Look also at the dear sun, the moon, and all the stars, how exactly they hold their course and carry out their vocation.[133]

Likewise, dear soul, every healthy human should also observe his calling, according to his station, with all diligence and earnestness. He should also teach, preach, govern, discipline, protect, keep house, build, improve, and care for his own as if he were to stay forever, and as if he were never to die; and this he shall do upon God's command and for the love of his offspring. In doing so, he shall live in such a way every day, maintain faith and preserve a good conscience, be ready at any moment for the blessed journey home,[134] and speak together with Saint Paul, THE TIME OF MY DEPARTURE IS AT HAND: I HAVE FOUGHT A GOOD FIGHT; I HAVE COMPLETED THE COURSE; I HAVE KEPT FAITH; HENCEFORTH, THE CROWN OF RIGHTEOUSNESS IS NEXT TO ME, WHICH THE LORD, THE JUST JUDGE, WILL GIVE TO ME ON THAT DAY; NOT ONLY TO ME ALONE, BUT ALSO TO EVERYONE WHO LOVES HIS PRESENCE.[135]

---

[129] Matthew 22.
[130] Ecclesiastes 6.
[131] John 5:17b.
[132] Hebrews 1:14.
[133] Psalms 8 and 19.
[134] 1st Timothy 1.
[135] 2nd Timothy 6b-8.

For that reason, dear soul, observe your vocation diligently as ordered by the Lord, so that you carry it out properly with all due patience and compassion.[136]

Make certain, however, to remain willingly at a lower standing; for that is better than everything sought by the world. If the Lord, however, elevates and promotes you, do not become proud; the higher you are, the more humble you shall become; for then the Lord will be fond of you, since he is a God of humility. WHO IS LIKE THE LORD OUR GOD, WHO IS SEATED SO HIGHLY, AND WHO DOES NEVERTHELESS BEHOLDS THE MEEK, BOTH IN HEAVEN AND ON EARTH?[137]

Do not seek a higher standing, and do not regard your own fortune, but always carry out what God has commanded.[138] For to him you shall give an account; that is why you should not be curious about what does not concern you; for you had been commanded more than you can carry out.

Also, do not involve yourself in matters of others, and do not attempt to affect concerns of God; do not presume to be clever enough, for such presumptions deceived many, and their foolhardiness has brought them down.[139] For it benefits you nothing to gawk at that which has not been commanded to you.

Also, do not become self-satisfied in your own affairs, and do not pride yourself when you are needed.[140]

And when you encounter affliction and discourtesy, take heart and persevere in carrying out your affairs; for how can he be aided who despairs in his affairs?

Be diligent in all things, and ask the Lord for blessing; for his blessing brings wealth without toil.[141] Many will grow tired

---

[136] Ephesians 4.

[137] Psalm 113:5-6.

[138] Sirach 3.

[139] Sirach 10 and 7 and 3.

[140] Sirach 10.

[141] Proverbs 10:22.

as they aim only at wealth and thereby obstruct only themselves.[142] He, however, who is weak and poor and much in need of help, shall remain calm; God looks upon him with mercy, and help him out of misery, and bring him to honor so that his own kind will be astonished.

Therefore, dear soul, persist in your vocation, and do not be fooled by how the ungodly seek fortune. Trust in GOD, and remain in your vocation. It is quite effortless for the Lords to make a poor person rich.

My Lord and my God! I know indeed that a human's actions are within his powers, and nobody controls how he carries on and where he directs his walk.[143] Govern me at all times through your Holy Spirit, so that I look straight ahead in my vocation, and that I faithfully await my turn. Guide me always on the righteous path, so that I waver neither to the right, nor to the left.

Affirm my course according to your word, and do not let injustice rule over me. Govern me always according to your contentment, for you are my God; may your good spirit lead me on an even path.[144] I know indeed, my God, that I am also called to your vineyard and that through my baptism I have promised to work for you.[145] I ask you that you give me a healthy body until my end; and strengthen me, so that I can willingly bear the load and the heat, and that I will always be faithful to you, my Lord.

Since the hour of my end is concealed from me, teach me to be ready at every hour and any moment,[146] so that I may have a blessed departure, to leave the world willingly, to fall asleep with peace and joy, and to observe the eternal holiday of rest together with you and with all the chosen people. Amen![147]

---

[142] Sirach 11.

[143] Jeremiah 10:23.

[144] Psalm 143.

[145] Matthew 20.

[146] Psalm 90.

[147] Luke 1.

6th Daily prayer.
The sixth article belonging to a
Christian life.

Sixthly: above all and more than anything else, dear soul, do not forget about the beloved prayer, for there is nothing more pitiful on earth than a person who does not pray and who does not talk to God. Yes, a person can give nothing to himself, unless it is given to him from heaven.[148] For all good gifts and all immaculate gifts come from above, from the Father of Light.[149] Prayer is like the cart on which we bring home the gifts of God. It is indeed like a little pipeline through which the blessing of the Lord flows toward us, both into our house and into our heart. For Scripture says this, THE PRAYER OF THE AFFLICTED PIERCES THROUGH THE CLOUDS, AND IT WILL NOT COME TO AN END UNTIL IT ARRIVES; AND IT WILL NOT CEASE UNTIL THE HIGHEST LOOKS UPON IT.[150]

Yes, dear soul, the beloved daily prayer is the most beautiful and heartfelt service which God desires from us daily. That is why he not only admonishes and commands us to pray often, contentedly, and without ceasing; he also gives us the most blissful promise that he will hear us and give us wholesome benevolence for body and soul.

This is his command: CALL ON ME IN AFFLICTION, AND I WILL RESCUE YOU, AND YOU SHALL PRAISE ME.[151] And also, ASK AND IT WILL BE GIVEN TO YOU; SEEK AND YOU WILL FIND; KNOCK AND THE DOOR WILL BE OPENED TO YOU.[152]

And this is his promise: TRULY, TRULY, I SAY TO YOU, IF YOU ASK SOMETHING OF THE FATHER IN MY NAME, HE WILL GIVE IT TO

---

[148] John 3.
[149] James 1:17a.
[150] Sirach 35:21.
[151] Psalm 50:15.
[152] Matthew 7:7.

YOU.[153] And also, IT WILL COME ABOUT; BEFORE THEY CALL I WILL ANSWER; WHILE THEY ARE YET SPEAKING I WILL HEAR.[154]

Behold, my soul, how your Lord has given you an example here on how to follow his footsteps. How often, how diligently, how willingly, how righteously he has prayed; how he has hurried into the desert so that he could be alone and pour out his heart in front of his father.[155]

He not only prayed for his own person, he also taught his beloved disciples to pray, and he provided them with the Lord's Prayer.[156] And therein he has provided to you and to all children of God the words with which to pronounce the great majesty of God.

And so that you have no excuse, he shows you how to step in front of God and in whose name to address God; "namely," says he, "in my name."[157] Indeed, raise your hands in the name of your savior Jesus Christ in true faith and in heartfelt confidence; and as true as Christ is your savior and sits at the right hand of his Father, indeed, as certainly will he also hear your prayer and all your lament.

Beyond all this, you shall also know which gifts to ask from God and how to distinguish them. Ask for temporal gifts under the condition of being God's will and of being good and blissful for you.[158] For the all-wise God knows best what his children need; and his sincerity will not provide any wicked and harmful gifts even if asked for in ignorance.[159] As his beloved children, we shall ask, desire, demand the spiritual gifts – which have been granted to us for our salvation and righteousness– of him assuredly and unconditionally as our merited and

---

[153] John 16:23b.

[154] Isaiah 65:24.

[155] Matthew 4.

[156] Matthew 6.

[157] John 16.

[158] Matthew 18; 1st John 5.

[159] Luke 11.

matured inheritance; namely, forgiveness of sins, righteousness, the Holy Spirit, and eternal life.[160]

Oh, dear soul, who would not be encouraged to pray; all our sighing will certainly be heard? Who would not want to seek; all good things are indeed to be found?[161] Who would not knock on the door; it will certainly be opened for him; indeed, receiving a welcome at which everything that is good for our body and soul is thrown into our lap? Therefore, dear soul, pray without ceasing throughout your life; call on the Lord in all your deeds; seek his help and advice in all your affliction; fear God, place your hope in God, trust in God, and await him – for mercy and comfort, blessedness and life will then be given to you at all times.[162] No one has ever been disgraced who trusted in God and who called on his name. FOR THE LORD IS CLOSE TO ALL WHO CALL ON HIM; TO ALL WHO CALL ON HIM IN EARNEST, HE WILL DO WHAT THE GOD-FEARING DESIRE, AND HE HEARS THEIR CRYING, AND HE LENDS THEM A HAND.[163]

I thank you, my Lord and my God! I thank you for this indescribable kindness,[164] not only that you have commanded us to beseech your helpful name in all affliction,[165] but also that your fatherly, benign heart has so blissfully declared to hear us indeed, and always to provide for us at the right time everything that is wholesome and good for our body and for our soul.[166] Yes, my Lord! I thank you, that you have touched my heart, that you have let me recognize my sins, and that you have granted me heartfelt remorse; for I have been divinely saddened, but not to my detriment, FOR DIVINE GRIEF BRINGS FORTH A

---

[160] Matthew 6.

[161] Matthew 7.

[162] 1st Thessalonians 5; Sirach 2.

[163] Psalm 145:18-19.

[164] John 11.

[165] Psalm 10.

[166] John 14 and 16; Psalm 145.

REMORSE THAT EFFECTS SALVATION FOR WHICH NOBODY FEELS SOR-
ROW.[167]

I ask you, my God! pour out over me your Holy Spirit, the spirit of
prayer,[168] so that I always have passion and love for prayer, and that I
bend the knees of my heart daily in front of you, my most beloved
Father; you, the rightful Father over everything called children in
heaven and on earth.[169]

Help, that I draw near daily, and that I –comforted and with all confidence in the name of my Lord Jesus Christ– ask you, call on you,
speak to you in all affliction, just as a beloved child speaks to his beloved father. Grant me also always to raise my holy hands up to you
without anger and without doubt;[170] and steadfastly to trust that all
my prayer, all my sighing that emerges from my heart will be heard
indeed. Impart in me to bear patience when aid seems to vanish, and
to demand neither time nor measure, but to hold on and wait for your
hour.[171] FOR YOU DELIGHT IN THOSE WHO FEAR YOU AND WHO AWAIT
YOUR GOODNESS.[172] Govern me also through your Holy Spirit, so that
I commemorate daily and often my hour of dying, that I remain well
prepared at every hour, and that I ask you wholeheartedly at all times
for a blessed departure.

---

[167] 2nd Corinthians 7:10a.

[168] Zechariah 12:10.

[169] Ephesians 3:14-15.

[170] 1st Timothy 2:8.

[171] Habakkuk 2.

[172] Psalm 147:11.

The 4th Chapter.

**Describes how a Christian shall conduct himself
when God afflicts him with illness.**

I.

**How shall a Christian conduct himself when he
becomes ill?**

 You do not know, dear soul, whether God will let you fall ill,[1] or whether he will call you suddenly, without weakness of the body. This is why I have reminded you so often not to wait for penance until you fall ill,[2] but rather to stand ready daily in faith and health, so that you will not be found at any time in a state wherein you would not dare to be saved. Remember the foolish, drunk, rich man Nabal; how swiftly the Lord struck and killed him.[3] Do not forget the rich man, who had denied even the breadcrumbs that had fallen from his table to poor Lazarus; how rapidly his life ended.[4] Remember also the rich miser of whom the Lord says: He had resolved on account of his riches to live merrily for a long time and with good courage; suddenly, however, God said to him: YOU FOOL, THIS VERY NIGHT YOUR LIFE IS BEING DEMANDED OF YOU. AND THE THINGS YOU HAD PREPARED, WHOSE WILL THEY BE?[5] Behold also, dear soul, the daily example of how many people die suddenly, before they get ill. Truly, my soul, in front of God you are no better than they are, and you do not know what he may yet impose on you.

---

[1] God will not let all humans fall ill.

[2] Sirach 18.

[3] 1st Samuel 25.

[4] Luke 16.

[5] Luke 12:20.

When, however, the Lord does strike you with a physical illness, and when he lays you onto your bed to linger, learn to prepare for it.

1. Recognize the causes of your illness, namely, your sins.

2. Seek forgiveness of your sins and reconcile with God.

3. Call on your Lord for a merciful rescue, and let the congregation of God also pray for you.

4. Do not disregard proper care and medicine if it is available to you.

5. If the illness carries on, then practice treasured patience, and guard against impatience.

6. Always have the assured comfort within your heart that you are a beloved child of God even in the midst of great weakness and pain.

7. When Satan dares you, oppose him in faith, and he will depart from you.

8. When the hour does arrive, surrender obediently.

9. And when the Lord does restore you, thank him wholeheartedly.

Safeguard me, my Lord Jesus! safeguard me from a wicked and hurried death, and do not let me die in my sins. Grant me, however, to commemorate my hour day and night, to stand ready at all times in true penance, in strong faith, and in firm hope, so that I may be awake with you and then fall asleep blissfully as you desire. And if it pleases you to strike me with bodily weakness – here I am; I know that you are sincere and kind, and that you do not lay anything on me that is not good and blissful for me.[6] Grant me, however, to be well prepared and to be a patient whose illness will serve to your honor. Amen![7]

---

[6] Romans 8.

[7] John 9.

II.

Explain to me now the aforementioned nine measures, so that I will properly learn how to behave in my illness.

1ˢᵗ Illnesses are God's rods.

Firstly, dear soul, bear well in mind, just as death itself is payment for the sins, so is also all illness punishment of God with which he strikes us for our misdeeds.[8] Do not act, dear soul, like the disbelieving, ungodly misers who, when they get ill, raise a hue and cry and worry only about their wherewithal now being finished without ability to acquire more; or they brood and ponder where they may have eaten an unhealthy bite, or where they had a harmful drink, or what else may have been done to them to cause the illness. Instead, bear in mind firstly what the prophet has said: IT IS THE FAULT OF YOUR WICKEDNESS THAT YOU ARE BEING CHASTISED LIKE THIS, AND OF YOUR DISOBEDIENCE THAT YOU ARE BEING PUNISHED LIKE THIS; THEREFORE, YOU MUST REALIZE AND ENDURE, WHAT KIND OF SORROW AND HEARTACHE IS CAUSED BY LEAVING THE LORD YOUR GOD AND BY NOT FEARING HIM,[9] as says the Lord Zebaoth.[10] And Sirach says, WHOEVER SINS IN FRONT OF HIS CREATOR, HE MUST ENCOUNTER THE HANDS OF THE PHYSICIAN.[11]

Do you hear that my soul? This you must observe in particular: when God intends something, and when he will strike us, all outward means must be readied for that. For when we humans do not want to recognize the illness of our souls, then God will let us fall ill in our bodies, so that we will bear in mind also our souls, and that we will initiate penance.

Yes, dear soul, just like our children deserve the chastising-rod, so do we deserve the punishment of illnesses from our

---

[8] Romans 8.

[9] Jeremiah 2:17, 19.

[10] Zebaoth: *host of heavens*.

[11] Sirach 38:15.

God. Oh, you pious God! if you would strike us with illness each time we encumber guilt, we would not enjoy health for one moment. You chastise us only occasionally, so that we will always remember, and that we shall fear your name.

GOD will often chastise the small, young, and innocent as well, so that it will hurt the elders and urge us to do penance.[12] Behold, my soul, illnesses are like messengers sent from God, calling on us to refrain from sins and to do penance, so that we do not perish in sin.

Keep in mind, dear soul, how deceptively secure some humans live from day to day, without hardship, without illness.[13] They have no regard for God's word, or for his sacraments; they forget about faith in Christ and endearing prayer; and thereby, their souls stand in great danger; the less a father chastises, the more the children's disobedience will get out of hand; therefore, the more humans enjoy health and prosperity, the more falsely secure they become.

Lord Jesus Christ! Here I lie in my illness, and I recognize that this is your fatherly will. Since I will lose not even one hair from my head without your will,[14] how shall I lose the precious gift of my health if not because of your will? Behold, my God! You have made me as it pleased you. And just as you, in your suffering, have become an egregious being and not a human[15]; so you created me also. My God! When you chastise a human for his sin, then his beauty is being consumed as if by moths.[16] I thank you for your chastisement, my God! And I am certain, that you bear no ill intentions.[17] My Lord! you are indeed a companion of humanity; the wounds inflicted by a friend, however, are well meant.[18] Therefore, I am certain that this illness will

---

[12] 2ⁿᵈ Samuel 12.

[13] Psalm 36.

[14] Luke 21; Matthew 10.

[15] Psalm 22:6.

[16] Psalm 39:11.

[17] Psalm 119.

[18] Proverbs 27:6.

also serve me for the better.[19] Whoever you love, you chastise.[20] Therefore, I am pleased that you chastise and humble me, so that I learn your laws. Help, my God! that I bear in mind this chastising-rod of yours for all my life, and that I be wary of sins, so that nothing dire will happen to me. Amen![21]

2nd Penance is the soul's health.

 Secondly: since you, dear soul, now feel through your physical illness that your soul has become ill for lack of penance, work foremost toward having your soul become healthy. The health of the soul, however, lies in true penance; in true faith in Jesus Christ through whom you reach the forgiveness of your sins and a merciful Father in heaven. For through faith you are being reconciled with God; you become righteous in front of him; and you find peace and joy in your conscience.[22] And thus your soul has healed, even if your body is still sick and very weak.

I confess to you, my Lord Jesus! with a shattered and crushed heart, I have indeed earned this illness with my sins, and I am wholeheartedly sorry to have angered your majesty, and to have brought myself into such misfortune. My God and my Lord! you do not disdain my troubled and crushed heart.[23] Look at my affliction and heal my broken heart.[24] Forgive me all my sins, and cleanse me of all my misdeeds with which I have enraged you. Lord, my Savior! you spoke so comfortingly to the troubled paralytic, comfort my soul as well, and speak into my heart this joyful word: BE COMFORTED, MY CHILD; ALL YOUR SINS ARE BEING FORGIVEN.[25] Oh, how lovely, how soothing this word is to my heart; how well it restores my body and soul, my marrow and

---

[19] Romans 5.

[20] Proverbs 3:12.

[21] John 5.

[22] Romans 5.

[23] Psalm 51.

[24] Psalm 147.

[25] Matthew 9:2b.

bone. Yes, Lord Jesus! if your holy word and promise of mercy would not be my comfort, then I would have to expire in my affliction.²⁶ I believe and I am certain indeed, that through you, Lord Jesus! I have forgiveness of all my sins, that I am well taken care of with my God, and that I am an heir of eternal salvation. Amen!

3ʳᵈ One shall ask God for rescue.

Thirdly: call on the Lord your God for rescue, and beseech him, that he will make you healthy again. For this says Sirach: MY CHILD, WHEN YOU ARE ILL, DO NOT DISREGARD THIS, BUT ASK THE LORD, AND HE WILL MAKE YOU HEALTHY.²⁷ Make known also all the affliction to the entire congregation of the church, so that the congregation will help you to call on God. For this says the Lord, WHEN TWO OF YOU BECOME ONE ON EARTH; WHATEVER THEY ASK FOR, THAT WILL BE DONE TO THEM BY MY FATHER IN HEAVEN; FOR WHERE TWO OR THREE ARE GATHERED IN MY NAME, THERE I AM IN THEIR MIDST.²⁸

Even if you, my soul, are too weak to pray with your mouth, let grief pour out of your faithful heart; for these two are strong and mighty; they are beyond words, and they do not come to an end, until the Lord looks upon for rescue.²⁹

Lord Jesus Christ! you have sent your messenger to me, namely this illness, admonishing me to do penance. Behold, my Lord! I recognize your good will, I am obedient, and I turn toward you. My God! I send a messenger back to you, namely my poor prayer and my sighing. Oh, Lord! accept my pleading and let my sighing come before you; if it pleases you, my Redeemer! and if it be blessedly granted that I

---

²⁶ Psalm 119:92.
²⁷ Sirach 38:9.
²⁸ Matthew 18:19b-20.
²⁹ Romans 8; Sirach 35.

live, ah, so help me stand up again to a new, healthy, Christian life until my end. If it does not please you that I live, but that the end shall come, ah, may it come swiftly, Lord Jesus! and take my soul into your hands. Amen!

4ᵗʰ Proper care is not to be disregarded.

Fourthly, dear soul, you are allowed to make use of proper medicine and care. For the wise man says also this, THEN LET THE PHYSICIAN COME TO YOU, FOR THE LORD HAS CREATED HIM; AND DO NOT LET HIM GO WHILE YOU STILL NEED HIS CARE.[30] Beware, however, dear soul, do not seek the physicians before you seek the Lord. King Asa did this in his illness; therefore, the Lord did not bless his medicine, and King Asa had to die.[31]

Also, do not employ forbidden means, and do not seek counsel of those who want to speak a blessing in the devil's name, trying to offer aid by abusing the godly name. For King Ahasia did this, seeking help from Baal-Zebub of Ekron, the idol. That is why the Lord said to him, IS THERE NO GOD OF IS-RAEL INDEED, SO THAT YOU GO AHEAD AND ASK FOR BAAL-ZEBUB, THE GOD OF EKRON? THEREFORE YOU SHALL NOT GET UP FROM THE BED ON WHICH YOU LAID YOURSELF, BUT YOU SHALL DIE.[32]

In particular, my soul, be cautious also of uneducated and uninformed physicians who have not learned their craft. For the human body is a precious creation of God; it shall be held in honor and not be depraved.

I thank you, my Lord Jesus Christ, you devoted physician of my soul,[33] that you have helped my sick soul, that you have cleansed it from sin, and that you have restored my heart with the medicine of living comfort. I ask you, oh, Creator of all things! bless also this ex-

---

[30] Sirach 38:12.

[31] 2nd Chronicles 16.

[32] 2nd Kings 1:16b.

[33] Exodus 15.

ternal medicine and the proper care that you have created. Lord! if it is your will, let it be wholesome to me and aid my health.[34] If, however, it is not your will, let it not benefit me. Lord, here I am, carry out with me what is pleasing to you and what is good and blessed for me. Amen!

5th Patience is a precious herb in illness.

Fifthly, dear soul, apply yourself to endearing patience and ask your God to safeguard you from impatience. Oh, it is exquisite to be patient, and to hope for the goodness of the Lord, for his kindheartedness is new every morning, and his devotion is great.[35] Look at your Savior Jesus Christ, and follow his example; how very patient was he in all his suffering.[36] Indeed, my soul, act like our children; when their head hurts, they come, they complain to their mother, they lay their hurting head into her lap, and they ask for help. Do alike, dear soul; complain to the Lord, throw your concern into his lap, and wait patiently for his help.[37]

Protect yourself meticulously from impatience. For impatience spoils everything; it angers God, the Lord; it prevents prayer, and it makes the illness even longer and more difficult. Endearing patience is a precious, healing herb; impatience, however, is poison to the heart.

Take away, Lord Jesus! and remove all impatience from my heart. Protect me at all times from impatience getting out of hand so that I do not make my affliction even greater. Plant, however, endearing, beautiful patience into my heart, so that I will follow your example, that I become quiet and patient, and that I wait for your help. Prompt your pointer of time. Let your hour come: for your time is the right time, and your hour is the right hour. Grant me to I hope steadfastly and to remain strong with assured confidence in your faithfulness;

---

[34] Matthew 8.
[35] Lamentations 3:22b-23.
[36] 1st Peter 2:21.
[37] Psalm 55.

you are faithful, and you do not let any human be tried beyond his ability.[38] Ah, my Lord Jesus! bring about also an end to all my affliction and illness, an end that I can bear. I know you will not fail. Amen!

6th Comfort in prolonged illness.

Sixthly, dear soul, if your illness lasts for a longer time than you have expected, do not think that the Lord has forgotten you; be assured that –even in the midst of affliction and illness– you are a beloved child of God and an heir of eternal life. For just as a mother cannot forget about her sick child, so does the Lord Jesus also not forget about you; for he has engraved you into the palms of his hands.[39] Indeed, my soul, the more a child is ill, the greater is the love which the mother bears toward it, and the greater is the care which she gives; so does the Lord your God act toward you; he gives you this comfort into your heart, saying, ARE YOU NOT MY PRECIOUS SON, AND MY BELOVED CHILD? I REMEMBER WELL WHAT I HAVE TOLD YOU; THEREFORE, MY HEART YEARNS FOR YOU, SO THAT I HAVE GREAT COMPASSION FOR YOU.[40] And also, AS A FATHER HAS COMPASSION FOR HIS CHILDREN, SO THE LORD HAS COMPASSION FOR THOSE WHO FEAR HIM.[41]

Lord Jesus, my Savior! I am complaining to you, for my affliction is burdening me, and my illness has lasted for a long time. I ask you, oh you - the essential word of your Father, you – the heavenly issuer of comfort, do voice this comfort deeply into my heart: that I am your beloved child at all times –even in the midst of greatest weakness, even in severe pain, and even in fright of death–, that I lie in your arms on your lap, and that I remain in your gracious sight at all times.

Indeed, Lord Jesus! as you were hanging on the Holy Cross, as you have borne our pain, shame, and humiliation, aban-

---

[38] 1st Corinthians 10:13.

[39] Isaiah 49:16a.

[40] Jeremiah 31:20.

[41] Psalm 103:13.

doned by all creatures, you were still the only begotten son of your heavenly Father, and you endured. When beloved Joseph lingered in prison, and when he saw no fountain of human help, you were still with him; you loved him; and you rescued him at the right time.[42] When Stephen was led to his death, and when stones were flying around his head, you loved him indeed; you gave him the vision, so that he could say with a joyful heart, BEHOLD ... I SEE THE HEAVENS OPENED, AND THE SON OF MAN IS STANDING AT THE RIGHT OF GOD.[43] When Lazarus lay in front of the door of the rich man, and when nobody wanted to help him, your angels were around him nevertheless; they took his soul, and they led him to lie in the lap of Abraham, into eternal paradise.[44]

Oh, my God! I am indeed also your Lazarus; I lie here, and I knock on your door with my grief. The affliction is quite severe indeed, my Lord! pain is abundant, and fear threatens to overwhelm me. I know for certain, however, –having a thousand witnesses in my heart through your Holy Spirit– that you will not leave me; day and night your eyes will remain opened above me; I am your beloved child and an heir of eternal life; for that is why you are with me in this affliction; you will tear me free and bring me to honor in this and the other life, as it pleases you; all this is indeed true. Amen![45]

7ᵗʰ Temptation.

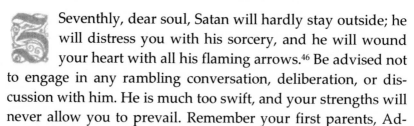 Seventhly, dear soul, Satan will hardly stay outside; he will distress you with his sorcery, and he will wound your heart with all his flaming arrows.[46] Be advised not to engage in any rambling conversation, deliberation, or discussion with him. He is much too swift, and your strengths will never allow you to prevail. Remember your first parents, Ad-

---

[42] Genesis 41.

[43] Acts 7:56.

[44] Luke 16.

[45] Psalm 91.

[46] Ephesians 6:16.

am and Eve. They were deceived by his trickery and deplorably seduced while they still were without sin and in possession of their unadulterated strength. How could you, miserable, impure sinner, persevere indeed?[47] Behold, however, your Lord Jesus Christ, and find comfort first in him, how he resisted temptation, overcome Satan for your benefit, and give his victory to you, so that Satan shall overpower you nevermore, no matter how severely he pursues you. Then behold also your Lord's example, how swiftly he dispatched of Satan with sayings of the divine word, and how he remained secure.[48] Therefore, pick up the sword of God's word also,[49] and withstand Satan steadfastly in faith; then he will depart from you.[50]

1st. When he says: your sins are greater than can be forgiven to you,[51] strike him with the true word of God; shout and repeat without ceasing: you lie, Satan, for it is written, WHERE SIN HAS BECOME MIGHTY, EVEN THERE MERCY HAS BECOME MUCH MIGHTIER.[52]

2nd. When he says: Christ's merits do not concern you; you do not belong to the number of the chosen, then shout without ceasing: you lie, Satan, for thus says my Lord Jesus: COME TO ME ALL WHO ARE AFFLICTED AND BURDENED, I WILL REFRESH YOU.[53] And also, AS THEY ALL DIE IN ADAM, SO WILL THEY ALL BE MADE ALIVE AGAIN IN CHRIST.[54]

3rd. When he describes to you how great the wrath of God is, then say without ceasing: FOR GOD SO LOVED THE WORLD ...[55] And also, BUT GOD DEMONSTRATED HIS OWN LOVE FOR US IN

---

[47] Genesis 3:1-24.

[48] Matthew 4:1-4.

[49] 1st Peter 5.

[50] James 4:7b.

[51] Genesis 3.

[52] Romans 5:20.

[53] Matthew 11:28.

[54] 1st Corinthians 15:22.

[55] John 3:16a.

THAT CHRIST DIED FOR US WHILE WE WERE STILL SINNERS.[56] And also, FATHER! YOU HAVE LOVED THEM EVEN AS YOU HAVE LOVED ME.[57]

4ᵗʰ. When he shows you the jaws of hell, then protect yourself with the word of God, and say, THE REASON THE SON OF GOD APPEARED WAS TO DESTROY THE DEVIL'S WORK.[58] And also, I WILL RELEASE THEM FROM HELL, AND RESCUE THEM FROM DEATH: DEATH, I WILL BE A POISON TO YOU; HELL, I WILL BE A PLAGUE TO YOU.[59]

5ᵗʰ. When he points out to you the weakness of your faith, then say, THE LORD WILL NOT ENTIRELY BREAK THE BRUISED REED, NOR EXTINGUISH THE SMOLDERING WICK.[60] And also, A BROKEN AND A CONTRITE HEART, GOD WILL NOT DESPISE.[61]

6ᵗʰ. When he says: you cannot pray, then answer: ah, but I can sigh, and while I know that this sighing of mine may be inarticulate, I know for certain that it will still penetrate through all the clouds.[62]

7ᵗʰ. When he says: your illness and suffering lasts long, God has forgotten you; then say, CAN A MOTHER FORGET HER CHILD AND HAVE NO COMPASSION ON THE SON SHE OF HER WOMB? AND THOUGH SHE MAY FORGET, I WILL NOT FORGET YOU; SEE, I HAVE ENGRAVED YOU ON THE PALMS OF MY HANDS,[63] speaks the Lord.

8ᵗʰ. When he says: you must perish in your poverty, for everyone has abandoned you; then say, FATHER AND MOTHER WILL ABANDON ME, BUT THE LORD WILL RECEIVE ME.[64] And also, AS LONG AS I HAVE MY LORD JESUS CHRIST, THEN I DO NOT ASK FOR ANYTHING IN HEAVEN AND EARTH; INDEED, EVEN IF MY BODY

---

[56] Romans 5:8.
[57] John 17:23b.
[58] 1ˢᵗ John 3:8b.
[59] Hosea 13:14.
[60] Isaiah 42:3.
[61] Psalm 51:17.
[62] Romans 8:26.
[63] Isaiah 49:15-16a.
[64] Psalm 27:10.

AND MY SOUL FAIL, THEN YOU, GOD! YOU ARE STILL MY HEART'S COMFORT AND MY PORTION FOREVER.[65]

9th. When he says: you must die nevertheless; then say, BLESSED ARE THE DEAD WHO DIE IN THE LORD FROM NOW ON.[66]

10th. When he says: you must be condemned nevertheless; then say with assurance, you lie, Satan, FOR ALL WHO BELIEVE IN THE LORD JESUS CHRIST SHALL NOT BE LOST, BUT SHALL HAVE ETERNAL LIFE.[67]

LORD Jesus Christ, you mighty vanquisher of evil and eternal Lord of victory! strengthen me in my weakness through your Holy Spirit, so that I grasp the armor of GOD when the wicked hour will come.[68] Place the shield of faith into the hand of my heart. Put on me the helmet of sacred hope, and place the sword of your word into my heart and mouth, so that I will resist rightfully by extinguishing the fiery arrows of the villain and by carrying out everything well – that I hold the battlefield and attain victory. Amen!

8th, 9th Death or Life.

Regarding eight and nine, dear soul, behold the end of your illness. When you see that your life shall continue no longer, then surrender patiently to the Lord; command your soul to him, speak assuredly at all times, and indeed, sigh with all your strength: LORD JESUS! RECEIVE MY SPIRIT![69] Then you will certainly not be lost, but saved eternally.

However, if he does raise you up again, then be grateful to him for the rest of your life, with all your heart, your words, and your deeds; and beware that you will not fare according to the old saying, after his recovery, the ill person became worse than he was before; instead, keep in mind the word of the LORD, saying, SEE, YOU ARE WELL AGAIN; STOP SINNING SO

---

[65] Psalm 73:26.
[66] Revelation 14:13b.
[67] John 3:16.
[68] Ephesians 6:11.
[69] Acts 7:59b.

THAT NOTHING WORSE WILL HAPPEN TO YOU.[70] **Fall on your knees and speak from the bottom of your heart:**

I thank you, Lord, almighty God! that you have struck me in a fatherly manner, that you have chastised me for the sake of my sins. Indeed, Lord! I am pleased that you have humiliated me so that I may learn your command.[71] Oh, my God! how often have I also thought of your servant, the King Hezekiah: NOW I WILL NO LONGER LOOK UPON HUMANS, OR BE WITH THOSE WHO NOW DWELL IN THIS WORLD; NOW MY TIME IS UP AND TAKEN FROM ME LIKE A SHEPHERD'S TENT. LIKE A WEAVER I HAVE ROLLED UP MY LIFE, AND HE HAS CUT ME OFF FROM THE LOOM; DAY AND NIGHT YOU MADE AN END OF ME.[72]

However, my GOD! I see that my illness' purpose was not for death, but for God's honor so that you, Lord Jesus Christ, shall be praised.[73] For you have found compassion with me, and you have kindheartedly accepted my soul. You tossed all my sins behind you, and you made my life last. How soundly you withdrew my illness, and how graciously you helped me.[74]

I thank you, my God! yes, I thank you from the bottom of my heart, that you have raised me up again, that you have strengthened me, so that I can visit the house of God again, that I can walk along my paths and trails, that I can carry out my deeds. It is because of your goodness, LORD! I would have otherwise ended long ago.[75] Oh, how often will I remember this chastising-rod, how much will I be ashamed throughout my life, and how I will beware from your wrath.[76]

Help me now, LORD my GOD! that I begin a new life with my new health. Grant me always to honor your name and always to have praise of you on my lips.[77] Govern me through your Holy Spirit, so

---

[70] John 5:14b.

[71] Psalm 119.

[72] Isaiah 38:11b-12.

[73] John 11; John 9.

[74] Isaiah 38.

[75] Ecclesiastes 3.

[76] Isaiah 38.

[77] Psalm 34:1.

that I live to your honor, and that I do not commit my limbs to being weapons of unrighteousness and serving sin,[78] but that they become weapons of righteousness[79] serving you, my GOD! that I sing your songs as long as I live, and that I praise and commend you in your congregation. Amen!

---

[78] Romans 6:13.
[79] Isaiah 38.

The 5th Chapter.

**Gives an account of various worldly and carnal notions
which may arise and which may often become
quite burdensome in the daily practice
of the art of dying.**

I.

**Whenever contemplating the hour of death, whether in ill-
ness or in health, a Christian's human heart will
naturally become frightened of death.**

 That is natural, dear soul, for our nature has initially
been created not for death, but for life. Death, however, has entered the world because of our sins, and
death is sins' wage and penalty.[1] Indeed, dear soul, just as
death is the destruction of living nature, so living nature is also
an enemy of death. Since humans are naturally fond of life, it is
no wonder –and also not sinful or distressing when being
scared of death– that humans take flight from death.

We do have a striking example in our Lord Jesus Christ,
who himself was frightened and scared of death.[2] Aside from
the many other profound causes for his grief and great fright at
the Mount of Olives, Jesus was also a true, natural human being with all the characteristics of our human nature. And when
God, the WORD, remained calm during the hour of such fright
of death and consented in profound obedience, and when he
endured such suffering, fear, and terror of physical death, there
was neither sinfulness nor dismay in his desire not to die. Indeed, he says on another occasion, I HAVE A BAPTISM WITH

---

[1] Romans 5 and 6.
[2] Matthew 26.

WHICH TO BE BAPTIZED, AND WHAT FEAR I SUFFER UNTIL IT IS COMPLETED.[3]

I thank you, Lord Jesus Christ! that you have not created me for death, but for life, and that you have engraved in my heart the love for life. I ask you from the bottom of my heart, teach me to keep in mind that death reigns over me for the sake of sins, and that death will finally strangle me. Grant me through your Holy Spirit –as often as death frightens me– to discard and resist all sin and to shun it always as death itself. Do help me to cling to you steadfastly with true faith – my Lord! who is life itself–, to overcome all fear of death,[4] and to say with comfort and joy, I WILL NOT DIE, EVEN WHEN I PERISH; BUT I WILL LIVE, AND I WILL PRAISE MY LORD.[5] Grant me to believe wholeheartedly that through you –the prince of life– I will be rescued from eternal death, and I shall attain righteous, eternal life. Amen!

II.
One still finds many people with a yearning desire for death.

Yes, indeed. There are, however, two kinds of people who wish for death: 1ˢᵗ. Unbelieving, heathen, ungodly hearts often wish their own death, but only from impatience caused by the great affliction with which God punishes them because of their sins. Since they are without cognizance of God and without true faith, they do not understand the meaning of Christ's suffering; they despair in impatience, they gripe against God, and they wish not only for death, but they often commit heedless suicide, like Judas, Saul, and Ahitophel.[6] They hope to end their misery or fright, but instead they obtain even more ever eternal misery and sorrow. Safeguard us from that, dear heavenly Father!

---

[3] Luke 12:50.
[4] John 11.
[5] Psalm 118:17.
[6] Matthew 27; Acts 1; 1ˢᵗ Samuel 31; 2ⁿᵈ Samuel 17.

2nd. The children of God themselves; the more their cognizance of God increases and their faith and love in Christ grows, the more they become weary of this wretched life, and the more they yearn for eternity. They always lament with our beloved Paul: I DESIRE TO DEPART AND BE WITH CHRIST.[7] The Lord himself has commanded them to pray and lament daily: REDEEM US FROM ALL EVIL.[8] Not only do they pray that God may release and rescue them from all worldly affliction of body and soul, but they also yearn wholeheartedly for final redemption: either for GOD to put an end to this wicked world, or for the blessed hour to come soon, indeed, and to bring eternal rest.

Help me, Lord Jesus Christ! to carry out well the mystery of your beloved plight, and to learn from you how to bear my yoke.[9] Guard me not to wish for death from impatience or for a shorter life than what you intended for me. Grant me, however, and bestow on me that I learn to know you, better and better, from day to day, that my faith will become stronger and stronger, and that I will grow even fonder of you over time; let me learn to despise this world and to seek the heavenly. Amen!

III.
May a human pray for a longer life
with a good conscience?

Saint Paul answers this question by pointing out that we are always supposed to honor Christ with our bodies, whether in life or in death. For (Paul says), CHRIST IS MY LIFE, AND DEATH IS MY GAIN. SINCE LIVING IN THE FLESH SERVES TO BE MORE FRUITFUL, I DON'T KNOW WHICH I SHALL CHOOSE, FOR I AM FOND OF BOTH: I DESIRE TO DEPART AND BE WITH CHRIST, WHICH WOULD ALSO BE QUITE PREFERABLE; BUT IT IS MORE NECESSARY TO REMAIN IN THE FLESH FOR THE SAKE OF YOU; AND WITH GOOD CONFIDENCE I KNOW THAT I WILL STAY

---

[7] Philippians 1:23b.

[8] Matthew 6:13b.

[9] Matthew 11.

AND REMAIN WITH YOU, SO THAT YOU IMPROVE AND REJOICE IN FAITH.[10]

You can hear, dear soul, how Saint Paul contemplates both: he longs for rest, regarding it even to be preferable; however, he also sees the merit in living longer; and he is confident that God will prolong his life, so that he can better serve God as well as humans. Either way, his goal is the same: giving praise in the name of Jesus, whether through life or through death.

King Hezekiah did likewise; when God's prophet had proclaimed that he would die, he cried and he asked the Lord to prolong his life for another fifteen years.[11] We also find that Saint Paul had greatly rejoiced after God had delivered his servant, Epaphroditus, from a deadly illness.[12]

Follow these examples, dear soul, then you will not fail, and you can be of service to GOD and to your neighbor; pray rightfully that GOD may prolong your life, that he may award you a healthy body, that he may lead you and govern you, so that you may become a vessel and a tool of graciousness. Surrender at all times to his will, and be prepared daily to leave this life, for the end is concealed from you.

ETERNAL, ALMIGHTY GOD! YOU ARE MY LIFE, AND MY TIME RESTS IN YOUR HANDS. FOR WITHIN YOU WE LIVE, WE MOVE, AND WE ARE.[13] I thank you from the bottom of my heart, that you have maintained me thus far, that you have given me a healthy body and a right mind, that you have put me into this profession and into this position in which I am able to serve you, my Lord, and my neighbor. My God! you see and you know my heart; that I am willing and ready to proceed faithfully in my profession, and that I have no evil intention within my heart. I ask you, if it is commendable to you and beneficial to me, prolong my life and guide me through your Holy Spirit, so that I will continue to live here to your honor; that I will learn to know your name

---

[10] Philippians 1:21-26.

[11] Isaiah 38.

[12] Philippians 2.

[13] Acts 17:28a.

better and better, that I will keep serving my neighbor more and more faithfully, and that I prepare my heart through true penance. If this, however, does not please you –and you do know better, oh, you wise God!– here I am; unharness me whenever you please; your will, my God! I shall carry out gladly. Amen![14]

IV.

By which motivation shall every single person surrender willingly to dying?

 By the obedience that is owed to his GOD. For we have our life from God; and God has the power to reclaim it from us. Nobody puts himself into this world, nor can anyone stay if it no longer pleases God. He lets humans die, saying, RETURN TO DUST, YOU MORTALS.[15]

Beware, dear soul that you will not die unwillingly when your hour has come, that you will not gripe against your God and say: I must die whether I want to or not. Thus behave the unbelievers, who have no hope and who trust in this life only; they will fare as the Lord has said, WHOEVER LOVES HIS LIFE WILL LOSE IT.[16]

You however, my soul, grant your Lord an obedient heart; live as long as he wishes, and die when he wishes. Let nothing deter you; let nothing in this world obstruct you; regard your life as nothing compared to the exuberant glory that shall be revealed to you.[17] Then it will be done to you as the Lord has said: WHOEVER HATES HIS LIFE IN THIS WORLD WILL KEEP IT FOR ETERNAL LIFE.[18]

Lord Jesus Christ! you were so willing and ready for your suffering, and you have become obedient to your Father unto death on the

---

[14] Psalm 40.
[15] Psalm 90:3b.
[16] John 12:25a.
[17] Romans 8:18.
[18] John 12:25b.

cross.[19] And you said: Father! NOT MY WILL, BUT YOUR WILL BE DONE.[20] I beseech you, my Savior! give me at all times an obedient heart and, when my hour has come, grant me to surrender willingly and to die gladly. Since you know my weakness, Lord! you know that flesh and blood are incapable of that. Lord! lead me according to your will, guide me in your footsteps. Grant that I completely trust you with body and life. My Lord, and my God! you most comforting Savior! you are good, and everything that you do is good; for you never had malevolent intentions, you never acted maliciously, and you never let anyone perish who placed his hopes in you. Here I am! Lord! within your hand of grace; if I live, then I live in you; if I die, then I die in you. Whether I live or die, I am yours.[21] And I will nevermore be lost, that is certainly true. Amen!

V.

It is nevertheless fair in this world, and its course is beautiful; who would not rather want to stay here.

All worldly children sing this song. You however, dear soul, do not associate yourself with the essence of this world.[22] Do not say that such is the world's course, but keep in mind that this course of the world leads straight into hell. For we are the children of saints; and we wait for another life that God will give to those who are strong in faith and who remain firmly with him.[23] Listen to what scripture says about the world's course, THE WHOLE WORLD (says Saint John) IS CONTROLLED BY THE EVIL ONE.[24] And also, DO NOT LOVE THE WORLD OR ANYTHING IN THE WORLD: IF ANYONE LOVES THE WORLD, LOVE FOR THE FATHER IS NOT IN THEM; FOR EVERY-

---

[19] Philippians 2:8.
[20] Luke 22:42b.
[21] Romans 14:8.
[22] Romans 12:2a.
[23] Tobias 3.
[24] 1st John 5:19b.

THING IN THE WORLD, NAMELY, THE LUST OF THE FLESH, THE LUST OF THE EYES, AND THE PRIDE OF LIFE, COMES NOT FROM THE FATHER BUT FROM THE WORLD; AND THE WORLD PASSES AWAY WITH ITS DESIRES: WHOEVER DOES THE WILL OF GOD, HOWEVER, WILL LIVE IN ETERNITY.[25] And also, ENTER THROUGH THE NARROW GATE, FOR THE GATE IS WIDE, AND THE PATH IS BROAD WHICH LEADS TO DAMNATION, AND MANY ENTER THROUGH IT; BUT THE PATH IS NARROW THAT LEADS TO LIFE, AND THERE ARE FEW WHO FIND IT.[26]

Listen, dear soul, to what this course of the world is, and see to where it leads, and keep in mind how very far it strays from the path of life. Call on the Lord, your GOD, that he would take you from this course of the world, and that he would set your feet onto the path of life.[27]

LORD Jesus Christ! open my ears, and teach my heart so that I receive such faithful warnings from you, and that I act accordingly. You do know me, my LORD! and you know how much my heart is latched onto the world, how easily it is led astray from the small path of life. Satan does not remain idle; he inflates the desires of the heart; he presents one opportunity after another for sin; and he postures in all kinds of ways, so that he would seduce and whisk away my soul. Oh, my Savior! enlighten my eyes, so that I will find your paths. Govern me through your Holy Spirit, so that I will not stray; steady my heart through the strength of faith, so that I remain firmly on the narrow road, and that neither sweet nor sour, neither affliction nor death, will have me veer off this road.[28] And whether body and life will remain in place or break up into a thousand pieces, help me to persevere and to attain the victory; grant me always to wrestle chivalrously and to thrust forward to you through death and life. Amen!

---

[25] 1st John 2:15-17.

[26] Matthew 7:13-14.

[27] Proverbs 3.

[28] Matthew 7.

VI.

No matter the circumstance, for him, who owns money and estate, who dwells in honor and glory, who lives in pleasure and joy, it will be difficult to leave everything behind when he shall depart.

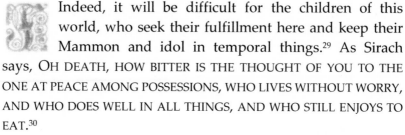 Indeed, it will be difficult for the children of this world, who seek their fulfillment here and keep their Mammon and idol in temporal things.[29] As Sirach says, OH DEATH, HOW BITTER IS THE THOUGHT OF YOU TO THE ONE AT PEACE AMONG POSSESSIONS, WHO LIVES WITHOUT WORRY, AND WHO DOES WELL IN ALL THINGS, AND WHO STILL ENJOYS TO EAT.[30]

For the children of God, however, that will certainly not be difficult; for even if they have been blessed by God and obtained money and estate, and even if they sit in high offices and stand in high honors and enjoy the benefits of the land with pleasure and joy,[31] they will still not be idolaters, attaching their hearts to their fortune; but they will thank God and use it well; and they know that these goods of the world matter only here, and that they are nothing before God.[32] Think continually about this word of the Lord, WHAT WOULD IT BENEFIT MAN IF HE INHERITED THE ENTIRE WORLD AND SUFFERED HARM TO HIS SOUL?[33]

Act likewise, dear soul; if you come to wealth, do not let your heart cling to it; if God places honors on you, be humble; if your standing creates joy, become not too self-assured.[34] Look at the examples of the saints: Abraham, Isaac, Jacob, Joseph, David, Daniel, etc., even Christ himself, and follow their footsteps; regard the Lord your God always as the highest good; be

---

[29] Psalm 17.
[30] Sirach 41:1.
[31] Isaiah 1.
[32] Psalm 62.
[33] Mark 8:36.
[34] Psalm 62.

comforted in his grace and rejoice in eternity; then you can forsake everything easily and freely at any time.[35]

Help me, my Lord Jesus Christ! to use all goods and splendors of this world as a pilgrim who is supposed to move on tomorrow.[36] Let my heart not desire more than the cherished daily bread for my sustenance. Grant me to be modest, and to make do, like a little lamb, even with less. Protect me, so that I will not create a mammon for myself and place my trust in the transitory and let it become an encumbrance during my hour of death. Help me, however, my Lord! and humble my heart, to choose the right and worthy part, namely you, my Lord! my Redeemer, my Savior! and let all my desire and joy be in you alone.[37] Bestow unto me to be wealthy only in my soul, to be heartfelt in faith, and to rejoice in you; then I have enough, both here temporally and there eternally; then I can willingly make peace with the world and leave joyfully and unencumbered from here. Amen!

VII.
It will be painful when a woman must leave behind her beloved husband, or a man his beloved wife and children, who are often left in poverty, without real trade and secure provisions.

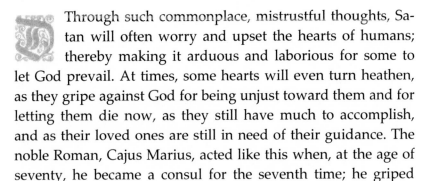 Through such commonplace, mistrustful thoughts, Satan will often worry and upset the hearts of humans; thereby making it arduous and laborious for some to let God prevail. At times, some hearts will even turn heathen, as they gripe against God for being unjust toward them and for letting them die now, as they still have much to accomplish, and as their loved ones are still in need of their guidance. The noble Roman, Cajus Marius, acted like this when, at the age of seventy, he became a consul for the seventh time; he griped

---

[35] 1st Peter 2.
[36] Psalm 39; Hebrews 11.
[37] Luke 10.

against his fate and god, and he complained about the injustice of having to die now, before carrying out all of his obligations.

The faithful children of God, however, do not behave like that; they know that they cannot be God to their loved ones; that they cannot even provide for them on their own; but that they are only housekeepers, assigned by God, to care of their loved ones for as long as it pleases him.[38]

And since they place their trust daily in the eternal, almighty, compassionate, all-knowing God and Father, they will look at no one else but him alone, they will dedicate and entrust everything to him, and they will find comforted assurance because he has assigned them to the office of housekeeper; and when he demands their departure, then he will also know well how to provide for the loved ones.[39] Indeed, he will become father and caretaker himself, as he so often has proclaimed in scripture; namely, to be the father of the widows and the helper of the orphaned. Scripture as well as daily experience confirm indeed that widows, widowers, and orphans are often being better provided for than during the lifetime of their beloved husbands, wives, and parents; for God neither deceives or lies nor sleeps or slumbers.[40] He pays attention to all and to everyone who call on his name; and he will never let himself be thought of as having neglected the welfare of some, for he looks upon the underprivileged both in heaven and on earth.[41] Indeed, dear soul, that is why he even allows the affliction of widows and orphans, so that his goodness will become great within them and his fatherliness be praised. For this is the certain foundation and assurance of all the afflicted: that he will provide for them, advise them, protect them, lead and guide them, if they accept him as their father; and no one will complain about him on that very day, that is certainly true.

---

[38] Luke 16.
[39] Luke 16.
[40] Psalm 121.
[41] Psalm 113.

Lord, my GOD! you have assigned me to the status of housekeeper (or lady-housekeeper), and you have committed me to supervise faithfully my loved ones; you know indeed, that I have executed this assignment by your grace –albeit in weakness– with all due diligence; that I have maintained my conscience, that I kept from unfaithfulness, and that I have supervised –as I would myself– all whom you have committed to me in both physical and spiritual things. I also have counseled them as I would wish to be counseled myself. Since I cannot maintain such care-taking any longer, since I am also ill and lie here in your mercy, I will now reassign this office back to you; perhaps you will carry it out better through another person.

My GOD! if my life is to be prolonged, then it shall be a Christian life; raise me up again, give me health and a good mind, so that I can supervise my loved ones even more diligently than before. If this is to be my end, however, may it be a blessed end. Here I am, I commit, I entrust, I surrender my loved ones altogether, the little as well as the big ones; may you be father, may you be mother, may you be the right caretaker; oh, you judge and father of widows and helper of orphans! YOU, GOD, SEE THE TROUBLE OF THE AFFLICTED; THE VICTIMS COMMIT THEMSELVES TO YOU; YOU ARE THE HELPER OF THE ORPHANS.[42] Now I will not interfere with your office; for my office now is to be prepared for the blessed journey home at any hour and moment, and to commit my soul to you. Your office is to take my place and be a father.

Lord Jesus Christ! you have assigned a caretaker for your beloved mother when she became one of the abandoned widows;[43] namely Saint John, the gospel writer; prepare and send good-hearted people also to my troubled widow to take care of her and those in need of loyalty and support.

Indeed, Lord Jesus! just as your mother became a widow, so have you also become an orphan; for your stepfather Joseph has not lived long; therefore, you know what it means to be a widow and an orphan; indeed, nothing is hidden from you; you know all matters of the heart!

---

[42] Psalm 10:14.
[43] John 19.

Oh, my Lord Jesus! you have become an orphan for the sake of all afflicted orphans; to you I commend my orphans – here they are; you will provide well for them, so that I and they will praise and thank you on the day of judgment.

Fulfill and bless their hearts at all times with righteous and true godliness; provide their bodies with consistent health, their lives with Christian chastity and honor; and award to them what will give them joy, here temporally and there eternally; and protect them from distress, here temporally and there eternally; satisfy them with a long life and show them your salvation.[44]

Indeed, my Refuge! you lead your loved ones wondrously.[45] Oh, teach and govern them at all times, so that they will wondrously follow you: give them patience and grace, so that their adherence will not cease, and that their faith and obedience will not end until you, hereafter, will bring them into eternal paradise. Amen!

VIII.
Say whatever you want, life is noble,
life is endearing.

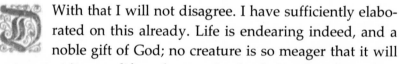 With that I will not disagree. I have sufficiently elaborated on this already. Life is endearing indeed, and a noble gift of God; no creature is so meager that it will not protect its own life and not resist death. You however, dear soul, must not love your life more than your creator; you must not regard this gift more than the Lord who has given it to you. You also must not forget that he has gained a much better life for you, and that he –through his ascension to heaven– has already assumed it to your benefit, which is concealed through Christ in God.[46] And when Christ –your life– will reveal himself, then you will also be revealed in eternal glory together with him.

---

[44] Psalm 91:16.

[45] Psalm 4.

[46] Colossians 3.

Since you, however, depend so much on this life, and since you love life far too much, I will have to confine it a little to show you what this life means, so that when you become weary in the future, you may yearn for eternity.

Listen to the patriarch Jacob, THE TIME OF MY PILGRIMAGE (says he) HAS LASTED ONE HUNDRED AND THIRTY YEARS; THE TIME OF MY LIFE IS SHORT AND WICKED, AND IT DOES NOT EXTEND TO THE TIME OF MY FATHERS AND THEIR PILGRIMAGES.[47]

And what does the often-tried man Job say about this? MUST NOT THE HUMAN (says he) ALWAYS BE QUARRELING ON EARTH, AND MUST HIS DAYS NOT BE LIKE THOSE OF A DAY LABORER? LIKE A SERVANT YEARNS FOR SHADE, AND A DAY LABORER YEARNS FOR AN END TO HIS WORK. SO I HAVE ALLOTTED MONTHS OF FUTILITY, AND NIGHTS OF MISERY HAVE BEEN ASSIGNED TO ME.[48] And again, MY DAYS ARE SWIFTER THAN A WEAVER'S SHUTTLE, AND THEY COME TO AN END WITHOUT HOPE.[49] And again, A HUMAN, BORN OF WOMAN, LIVES ONLY FOR A SHORT TIME, AND IS FULL OF DISQUIET; HE SPRINGS UP, LIKE A FLOWER, AND WITHERS AWAY; HE IS FLEETING LIKE A SHADOW, AND HE DOES NOT ENDURE.[50]

What says Moses, the man of God, in the 90th Psalm about it? OUR LIFE, says he, LASTS FOR SEVENTY YEARS; IF IT IS LONG, FOR EIGHTY YEARS; AND IF IT HAS BEEN EXQUISITE, IT WAS FULL OF TROUBLE AND TOIL; FOR IT PASSES BY QUICKLY, AS IF WE WOULD FLY AWAY.[51]

What says the royal prophet David about it? HUMANS (says he) ARE LIKE A BREATH; THEIR TIME IS LIKE A FLEETING SHADOW.[52]

What preaches Solomon about it? IN ALL THEIR LABORS (says he) IS SO MUCH TOIL, THAT IT IS TO NOBODY'S GAIN.[53] And also,

---

[47] Genesis 47:9b.

[48] Job 7:1-2.

[49] Job 7:6.

[50] Job 14:1-2.

[51] Psalm 90:10.

[52] Psalm 144:4b.

[53] Ecclesiastes 1:3.

WHAT DO PEOPLE GET FOR ALL THE TOIL AND ANXIOUS STRIVING WITH WHICH THEY LABOR UNDER THE SUN?[54]

What do the beloved old church teachers think about it? Saint Augustine says this: MY LIFE IS A MISERABLE LIFE; A MEAGER LIFE; THE OLDER IT GETS, THE MORE IT DECREASES; THE FURTHER IT EXTENDS, THE CLOSER IT COMES TO DEATH: IT IS A DECEIVING AND A TRANSITORY LIFE, FULL OF ROPES OF DEATH.[55]

And again, OH LORD! HOW WEARY AM I OF THIS LIFE, AND OF THIS ARDUOUS PILGRIMAGE; FOR IT IS A MISERABLE LIFE, AN INCONSISTENT LIFE, AN UNCERTAIN LIFE, A LABORIOUS LIFE, AN IMPURE LIFE, A LIFE WHEREIN THE WICKED RULE, AND THE CONCEITED HAVE THE POWER; IT IS FULL OF TRIBULATION AND DECEPTION, AND IT SHOULD NOT BE CALLED LIFE, BUT DEATH; WHEREIN WHICH WE DIE AT ALL TIMES FROM VARIOUS ILLNESSES AND INFIRMITIES, WE DIE IN VARIOUS MANNERS AT ANY MOMENT.

Keep in mind here, dear soul, how the saints and the children of God have always regarded this miserable life, and how they have become weary of it from very early on. If you still love life so much, and if you still think highly of it, then you indicate that you are worldly-minded, that sinful desires govern you even now, and that not much of God's cognizance and only little penance and faith must be in your heart. Oh, think more highly, dear soul, be not so bodily-minded, seek that which is above, and not that which is on earth.[56] If you have been resurrected with Christ, then seek what is above – where Christ is, sitting to the right of God.

LORD Jesus Christ, my God and my Salvation! I confess to you, indeed, and grieve over my decayed flesh and blood; that I am so worldly-minded, and that I love the transitory existence of this life far too much. I ask you, my God! enlighten my eyes, so that I look at this life rightly, that I regard its misery and vanity, that I recognize its dangerous difficulties. Strengthen me, my God! through your Holy Spirit, so

---

[54] Ecclesiastes 2:22.

[55] Augustine, *De Beata Vita* 4.25.

[56] Colossians 3:2.

that I restrain my flesh and blood, rein in my yearnings, and numb my desires; grant me, that I regard everything which is transitory as unworthy, and all joys of this world as bitter. Do plant inside me the yearning for the everlasting, and let me sense the taste of the eternal, so that I become weary of this miserable life, that I yearn for death, and that I may become certain of eternal life in my heart. Amen!

HERR JEsu Christe / mein GOtt und mein Heil! Ich bekenne dir ja und klage über mein verderbtes Fleisch und Blut / daß ich so gar irrdisch gesinnet bin / und das vergängliche Wesen dieses Lebens viel zu lieb habe: Ich bitte dich / mein GOtt / erleuchte mir meine Augen / daß ich diß Leben recht ansehe / sein Elend und Eitelkeit betrachte / und seine gefährliche Mühseligkeit erkenne. Stärcke mich / mein GOtt! durch deinen heiligen Geist / daß ich mein Fleisch und Blut zwinge / meine Begierden dämpffe / meine Lüste übertäube! Gib / daß mir alles Vergängliche unwerth / und aller Freuden dieser Welt bitter seyn. Pflantze aber in mich die Begierden des Unvergänglichen / und laß mich empfinden den Vorschmack des Ewigen / auff daß ich dieses elenden Lebens überdrüssig / des Todes begierig / und des ewigen Lebens in meinem Hertzen gewiß seyn möge. Amen!

Das VI. Capitel.

Berichtet wie ein Christen-Mensch sich freudig und frölich zum Sterben ergeben / alle Bitterkeit des Todes überwinden / und in gläubiger Beständigkeit biß ans Ende verharren könne und soll.

I.

Sage mir nun / womit soll und kan ich die Furcht des Todes stillen / daß ich mich meinem GOtt gantz freudig und frölich ergebe?

VOr Zeiten lehreten die heidnischen Gelehrten: Es wäre kein besser Raht / wenn es zum Sterben käme / als daß man einen frischen Muht fassete / den Tod verachtete / und gedächte / es könne nun nicht anders seyn / es wäre nur ein böß Stündlein zu thun / so wäre es aus. Solches hielten sie für eine grosse Kunst und Weißheit. Also that jener heidnischer König Agag / da er sahe / daß ihn der Prophet Samuel zu Stücken hauen wolte / ginge er ihm getrost / und sprach: Also muß man des Todes Bitterkeit vertreiben / 1 Sam. 15.

Desgleichen hören wir noch heutiges Tages / offt auch von denen / die sich gute Christen rühmen / wenn man vom Tode redet / rümpffen sie sich / sprechen: Es gehöre einen Muht dazu / es sey nur eine böse Stunde zu thun.

Aber / liebe Seele / das sind fleischliche Gedancken / und ein erdichteter Muht bringet keinen Trost in das Hertz / und hat keine Hoffnung des ewigen Lebens / ihr Hertz ist voll Schrecken und Angst / und wissen ihre Seele niemand zu befehlen.

Dagegen aber haben die gläubigen Kinder Gottes viel eine bessere Artzney wider des Todes Furcht / nur eine gewisse Kunst / die vom Himmel geoffenbahret ist / nemlich / den wahren Glauben / und hertzliche Zuversicht zu unserm HErrn JEsu Christo: Wer den hat / und sich an ihn hält / der hat die rechte eigentliche Artzney wider den Tod / und wider alle seine Bitterkeit. Ja / meine Seele / was woltest du den Tod fürchten? Weissest du doch wol / wer du bist / und was du bist. Warlich / du bist theuer erkaufft / was zitterst du für dem Tode? Siehe / Christus ist dein Leben / Phil. 1. Was zagest du? Sterben ist dein Gewinn. Weissest du nicht wohin? Sihe / Christus ist der Weg und die Leiter zum Himmel / Joh. 14. Weil du den hast / so kan dir kein Tod schaden / weil du Christum hast / kanst du nicht verlieren / ob schon Leib und Leben auffgehet / denn Christus stehet für dir in alles.

JA / mein HErr JEsu Christe! du bist für mich gestorben / du hast mir deinen Vater versöhnet / du hast meine Sünde gebüsset / du hast den Tod verschlungen / und mir das ewige Leben erworben. Solches gläube ich von Hertzen / und halte mich an dich fästiglich / darum habe ich in meinem Hertzen Friede und Freude / Trost und Wonne / und achte des Todes nicht. Ja / HErr JEsu! durch dich habe ich Vergebung aller meiner Sünden / bin für GOtt gerecht und rein / bin an ihm ein gnädigen lieben Vater / bin sein liebes Kind / und Erbe seines Himmelreichs. Mein HERR JEsu! ich bin dein Eigenthum / du hast mich erkaufft mit deinem Blut / und erlöset aus der Höllen: Ja / du bist mein Bruder / und ich dein Mit-Erbe / denn alles / was du hast / das ist auch

The 6th Chapter.

Gives an account of how a Christian can and shall surrender joyfully and cheerfully to dying, overcome all bitterness of death, and endure in faithful steadfastness until the end.

I.

Tell me now, how should and how may I silence the fear of death, so that I will surrender joyfully and cheerfully to my God?

 In ancient times, the heathen scholars taught that there is no better council when it comes to dying than to gather renewed courage, to despise death, to face the awful hour, and to find the unavoidable end. They regarded this to be a great skill and wisdom. The heathen king, Agag, thought this when the prophet Samuel prepared to put him to death; Agag went to him calmly, saying, THUS, THE BITTERNESS OF DEATH IS DISPELLED.[1]

This we still hear today, often even from those who claim to be good Christians; when they talk of death, they squirm and say that special courage is required during that awful hour.

However, dear soul, such thoughts are commonplace; false courage brings no comfort to the heart and offers no hope for eternal life; these hearts are scared and frightful, and their souls are committed to no one.

The faithful children of God, however, have a much better remedy against the fear of death; they even have an assured practice revealed from heaven; namely, true faith and heartfelt confidence in our Lord Jesus Christ. Whoever has him and whoever clings to him has the rightful, true remedy against

---

[1] 1 Samuel 15:32b.

death and against all its bitterness. Indeed, my soul, why would you fear death? You are fully aware of who you are, and what you are. Truly, you have been purchased at a high price; why do you tremble because of death? Behold, Christ is your life.[2] Why do you despair? Death is your gain. Do you not know where to go? Behold, Christ is the way and the ladder to heaven.[3] Because you have him, death will not harm you; because you have Christ, you cannot be defeated even if body and life fade away, for Christ endured everything for you.

Yes, my Lord Jesus Christ! you died for me, you have reconciled me with your Father, you have purged my sins, you have devoured death, and you have attained eternal life for me. This I believe with all my heart, and I cling to you firmly; therefore, I have peace and joy in my heart, I have comfort and delight, and I do not look upon death. Indeed, Lord Jesus! through you I have the forgiveness of all my sins, I am righteous and pure before God, I have a merciful dear father, and I am his beloved child and heir of his heavenly kingdom. My LORD Jesus! I am your property, for you have purchased me with your blood, and you redeemed me from hell. Yes, you are my brother, and I am your joint heir; for everything that you have is also mine; indeed, I am your dearest bride, your desire and joy, your treasure, which you have purchased for a high price. Furthermore, I am a temple and dwelling of your Holy Spirit, through whom I am confirmed and assured in faith. Yes, the Holy Spirit has connected me, united me with you, my Lord! and so firmly tied to you that I am bone of your bone and flesh of your flesh; and all creatures would have to perish before anything can separate me from your love.[4] What can death do to me? Truly nothing more than bringing me closer to you, my LORD Jesus! Therefore, I regard death as nothing; I have life in my heart, and I speak of nothing but of life: for Christ is my life, and death is my gain.[5] Indeed, I sing and say with beloved Job, I KNOW THAT MY RE-

---

[2] Philippians 1.

[3] John 14:6.

[4] Romans 8.

[5] Philippians 1:21.

DEEMER LIVES, AND THAT IN THE END HE WILL STAND ON THE EARTH, AND AFTER MY SKIN HAS BEEN DESTROYED, YET IN MY FLESH I WILL SEE GOD; HIMSELF I WILL SEE AND MY EYES WILL LOOK UPON HIM; I, AND NOT A STRANGER.[6]

Lord Jesus Christ! you know that I believe in you, and that I firmly cling to you with this faith of mine: I know also, that I believe in you, and that I find the sweetness of your comfort, even the taste of eternal life in my heart.[7] You are within me, and I am within you; everything that is yours is also mine; namely, life, and eternal delight and joy. What concern do I have for the transitory? When I have you, then I have everything that pleases me, here, temporally, and there, eternally. Away with all passing desires, with all the glory of this life, and with all transitory things. LORD Jesus! you are my delight, you are my joy, you are my money, my estate, you are my honor, my fame, my glory, my desire, and my eternal wealth. HEARTILY, I LOVE YOU, LORD! MY STRENGTH, LORD! MY ROCK, MY FORTRESS, MY RESCUER, MY GOD, MY SHELTER, ON WHOM I TRUST; MY SHIELD AND BUGLE FOR MY SALVA-TION; AND MY PROTECTION.[8] IF I ONLY HAVE YOU, THEN I DO NOT ASK FOR HEAVEN AND EARTH; AND EVEN IF MY BODY AND SOUL PERISHES, SO ARE YOU, GOD! MY HEART'S COMFORT AND MY PORTION FOREVER.[9] My heart has taken in this faith, this love, this affection toward you, my LORD Jesus! and I am thus strengthened, so that I fear neither affliction nor death; for I am certain that all these things, even death itself, will WORK TOGETHER FOR GOOD.[10] Let the hour come, when it is your will; I know and I am certain that with you and through you I will have eternal life and complete fulfillment.

---

[6] Job 19:15-27a.
[7] 2nd Timothy1.
[8] Psalm 18:1-2.
[9] Psalm 73:25-26.
[10] Romans 8:28.

Come, Lord Christ / Come, you faithful God,
   And provide an end for me,
Strangle the last enemy, which is death,
   Lead me out of misery,
Bring me into the righteous fatherland,
For you have spent your blood for me,
   Let me journey home with joy,
A M E N.

II.

This will indeed bring life and comfort into the heart;
if only I could also persevere steadfastly,
so that my faith will endure.

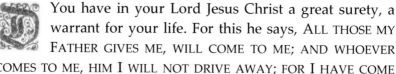 You have in your Lord Jesus Christ a great surety, a warrant for your life. For this he says, ALL THOSE MY FATHER GIVES ME, WILL COME TO ME; AND WHOEVER COMES TO ME, HIM I WILL NOT DRIVE AWAY; FOR I HAVE COME FROM HEAVEN, NOT TO DO MY WILL, BUT TO DO THE WILL OF HIM WHO SENT ME.[11] AND THIS IS THE WILL OF THE FATHER WHO HAS SENT ME, THAT I SHALL LOSE NONE OF ALL THOSE HE HAS GIVEN ME, BUT I RAISE THEM UP AT THE LAST DAY: THAT IS THE WILL OF HIM WHO HAS SENT ME, THAT WHOEVER SEES THE SON AND BE-LIEVES IN HIM SHALL HAVE ETERNAL LIFE, AND I WILL RAISE HIM UP AT THE LAST DAY.[12]

Do listen, dear soul, to the mouth of truth; what comforting words these are! how they delight heart and courage! With this, the Lord –who cannot lie– promises that your faith shall not end and that you shall not be lost, but permanently sustained until eternal life.

And the Lord says also, I HAVE PRAYED FOR YOU THAT YOUR FAITH SHALL NOT END.[13]

---

[11] John 6:36-37.
[12] John 6:39-40.
[13] Luke 22:32a.

And also, MY SHEEP HEAR MY VOICE, AND I KNOW THEM, AND THEY FOLLOW ME, AND I GIVE THEM ETERNAL LIFE; AND THEY SHALL NEVER PERISH, AND NO ONE WILL SNATCH THEM FROM MY HAND; THE FATHER WHO HAS GIVEN THEM TO ME IS GREATER THAN EVERYTHING, AND NO ONE WILL SNATCH THEM OUT OF MY FATHER'S HAND; I AND THE FATHER ARE ONE.[14] Likewise, he also says, MARY HAS CHOSEN THE GOOD PART; THAT SHALL NOT BE TAKEN AWAY FROM HER.[15]

Keep in mind, dear soul, how could the LORD safeguard you more beautifully than by promising and assuring you that he will make good his word through the power of his spirit, that your faith shall not cease, that no one shall snatch you out of his and his Father's hand, and that the good part –which you have in your heart– shall not be taken away from you. Therefore, you are now assured, my soul, not only of eternal life but also of your perseverance until eternal life; through his grace you will persevere enduringly until the end; he will not let go of you, and you will not let go of him.

Therefore, be comforted, and rejoice, and say together with Saint Paul, I KNOW IN WHOM I BELIEVE, AND I AM CERTAIN THAT HE WILL KEEP MY DEPOSIT SAFE FOR ME, UNTIL THAT DAY.[16] And also, I AM CERTAIN, THAT NEITHER DEATH NOR LIFE, NEITHER ANGELS NOR DEMONS, NOR ANY POWERS, NEITHER THE PRESENT NOR THE FUTURE, NEITHER HEIGHT NOR DEPTH, NOR ANY OTHER CREATURE, WILL BE ABLE TO SEPARATE ME FROM THE LOVE OF GOD, WHICH IS IN CHRIST JESUS, OUR LORD.[17]

LORD Jesus Christ! you alone are my righteous, my only, and my eternal part which I have chosen; and I am certain and assured within my heart that it will not be taken away from me.[18] Oh, you great surety, who can despair in you? Oh, you almighty shepherd, who can

---

[14] John 10:27-30.
[15] Luke 10:42b.
[16] 2 Timothy 1:12.
[17] Romans 8:38-39.
[18] Luke 10.

snatch me from your hand?[19] Oh, you loving Savior, who is love himself, who can separate me from your love? You are indeed mine, and I
am yours; you live in me, and I in you.[20] You have already ignited the
taste of eternal delight in my heart; and you have let me appreciate
glimpses of joy. Indeed, LORD Jesus! I feel the testimony of your Holy
Spirit within my heart –which gives witness to my spirit– that I am a
child of God and your joint heir in eternity.[21]

You are the vine, and I am the branch in you; you are the tree of
life, and I am firmly implanted in you through my living faith.[22] You
are the bridegroom, and I am your entrusted heart, betrothed to you,
united with you, linked to you through an indissoluble bond which
neither affliction, nor death, nor devil, nor fright, nor terror shall separate forever.[23] My Lord, my God, my shelter, my comfort, my desire;
you are the delight of my heart; you are the joy of all my strengths!
How my heart's desire burns for you! How can my heart adequately
delight in you? When will I get to the place where I can look upon
your comforting face?[24]

Oh, most beautiful, most pleasing, most beloved, most forthcoming
Lord! for you I live; for you I die; yours am I dead and alive; most certainly assured, confirmed, avowed, approved, persuaded in my heart,
that I am a chosen heir of eternal salvation. Praised be the Lord my
God, who has so soundly assured and comforted my soul. Amen.

---

[19] John 10.
[20] 1 John 4.
[21] Romans 8:16-17.
[22] John 15.
[23] Hosea 2:19.
[24] Psalm 42.

III.

What shall a Christian do if he does not always find such joyousness of faith, but instead great weakness, concern, and agitation, often questioning whether or not he is chosen for salvation?

He shall have no doubt, and he shall not cling to his physical weakness; but he shall keep in mind what the Lord said: THE KINGDOM OF HEAVEN HAS SUFFERED VIOLENCE, AND THOSE WHO ARE VIOLENT HAVE BEEN RAIDING IT.[25] Indeed, he shall keep in mind the admonition of Saint Paul, I REMIND YOU TO AWAKEN THE GIFT OF GOD, WHICH IS IN YOU. [26] May he also take comfort in the beneficial assurance spoken by the LORD, A BRUISED REED HE WILL NOT BREAK, AND A SMOLDERING WICK HE WILL NOT SNUFF OUT.[27] May he refresh his soul with the word of the Lord, saying, DON'T BE AFRAID, JUST BELIEVE.[28] And again speaks the Lord to the paralytic: TAKE HEART, MY SON; YOUR SINS ARE FORGIVEN.[29]

For, dear soul, daily experience shows: the more anyone keeps to God's word and contemplates the sayings of comfort, the more comfort will arise within the heart. Especially, however, when contemplating the sacred call of the Lord, and his friendly voice, COME TO ME, ALL YOU WHO ARE WEARY AND BURDENED, AND I WILL REFRESH YOU.[30]

Listen, my soul, how blissfully and pleasantly the Lord is calling you; how he beckons you, like a sitting hen her stray chicks, and like a devoted shepherd his lost sheep.[31] Keep in

---

[25] Matthew 11:12.

[26] 2nd Timothy 1:6.

[27] Isaiah 42:3.

[28] Mark 5.

[29] Matthew 9:3.

[30] Matthew 11:28.

[31] Matthew 23; John 10.

mind that you are now among the troubled and the burdened[32] to whom this voice of the LORD is directed. Answer the Lord, therefore, with an obedient, willingly believing heart, and surrender to the Lord with a contrite and frightened and shattered heart; that will please him, and he will not disdain it. As he has promised, I look at the humble and contrite, at him whose spirit is broken, and at him who fears my word.[33]

Do you not know, dear soul, that the Lord raises up those who are weak in faith?[34] For weak faith is also true faith, as long as you fight, wrestle, hold steadfast, not give up, and hold on to the word of promise. For thus speaks the treasured man, Dr. Martin Luther: If God does not keep his promise, our salvation is already done for: God, however, keeps his promise firmly, and he does not deceive. Therefore, even when our heart wavers, we find refuge in him who does not waver. For he says this, I AM THE LORD WHO DOES NOT DECEIVE. And also, GOD'S GIFTS AND CALLINGS CANNOT BE CHANGED.[35]

Keep this in mind, dear soul, and hold steadfastly to the word; let his word become certain, and even if your heart is discouraged, do not be frightened; for God is greater, and his word is much more certain than your own heart.[36]

However, do also learn the ways of the Lord; he delights in children of humankind,[37] he is tender and plays with them, like parents with their beloved children; sometimes he withdraws his protective hands a little; not for their detriment and downfall, but so they learn to trust not themselves, but God, the LORD, who can raise the dead and, indeed, strengthen the weak.[38]

---

[32] Psalm 51.

[33] Isaiah 66:2.

[34] Romans 14.

[35] Romans 11:29.

[36] 1ˢᵗ John 3:19-20.

[37] Proverbs 8.

[38] 1ˢᵗ Corinthians 1.

He does not delight in presumptuousness, but he wants us to serve him with fear and celebrate his rule with trembling.[39] How the presumptuous fare, when they build on their own courage and strength, can be seen with Saint Peter and beloved Thomas.[40] No one rightfully knows himself; we are revealed to God alone. That is why you shall always pray to God for merciful governance and maintenance until the end; and be assured, if you have ever felt comfort, it will surely come again; if the Lord has ever pleased your heart, he will surely do it more often. Indeed, even if you have not received one spark of comfort throughout your life, do not despair; pray, believe, hope, be patient; the comfort of the LORD will certainly come, and it will not remain outside, especially not during your very end.[41]

Keep in mind the example of the Canaanite woman;[42] behold, how tender the Lord was with her; indeed, how he guided her three times: the first time he remained completely silent, and he did not answer a word; the second time he said that he has not come for the good of her, but for that of the children of Israel; the third time he likens her to a dog unworthy of his comfort. And what does she do? Firstly, in response to his silence, she puts forth a patient heart that has learned well to hope and to wait. Secondly, she responds to the Lord by putting forth a firmly believing heart which is also veiled in the word and which wants to partake in the promise. Thirdly, she responds to him with a humble heart: that she would gladly be likened to a dog, desiring only the crumbs that fall from the table; that is, receiving only meager help and only the smallest spark of comfort, being quite sufficient for her and for her daughter. Finally, the Lord does not hold back any longer; he

---

[39] Psalm 2:11.
[40] Matthew 16; John 20.
[41] Habakkuk 2.
[42] Matthew 15.

even pours out the full barrel of his help, saying, WOMAN, YOU HAVE GREAT FAITH. MAY IT HAPPEN AS YOU REQUESTED.[43]

You may say: sure, she was strong in faith, but I am all too weak. Then, be aware that our faith is like a wrestler who is always worried about losing and being too weak to overcome his opponent. Our faith is likewise: when it wrestles and fights, we think it much too weak and easily defeated in the contest; but on the contrary: victory belongs to faith, no matter the circumstance; victory belongs to faith, even if it is weak; for faith shall hold the ground,[44] and it shall be kept safe for salvation through God's power.

Keep in mind also the fight of the patriarch Jacob, how he has wrestled with God, and how he persisted and not relented, saying, I WILL NOT LET YOU GO UNLESS YOU BLESS ME.[45] And then God blessed him.

LORD Jesus Christ, you do know that I believe in you, and although my faith is weak, I will place all my trust in you; stretch out to me your comforting hand and pull me toward you. My Lord, I am weak; oh, increase my faith;[46] oh, strengthen my trust. Do not be cruel to me, my refuge, for you are my only assurance; where else can I go? Ignite that little spark in my heart through your Holy Spirit; you see that I am willing, now see me through to completion.[47] Lord Jesus, you are my life, you are my comfort, you are my salvation; when I have you, then I have everything. I still hold on to you now, although only with a very weak hand; and the weaker my hand gets, the stronger yours becomes. Oh, do not let my hand slip from yours, so that I will not let go of you.

Now, Lord Jesus, behold and look at me, as you have looked at beloved Peter, beloved Mary Magdalene, the Canaanite woman, and

---

[43] Matthew 15:28.
[44] 1st Peter 1.
[45] Genesis 32:26.
[46] Luke 17:5b.
[47] Romans 7.

beloved patriarch Jacob;[48] chase away the darkness from my heart, and let a spark of your comfort ignite in me. Here I am, a poor little dog, and I await the breadcrumbs from your table of mercy; here I drift, a poor snail, in my misery, and I grasp at the heavenly dew. Behold, I wrestle with you like beloved Jacob; oh, you strong LORD, do yield to my heart; do yield, since you know well that the victory is mine; I will not let go of you unless you bless me;[49] I will not cease until the sun of your comfort rises for me.

LORD Jesus Christ, you have pleaded for beloved Peter that his faith shall not cease;[50] you sit indeed to the right hand of your father, and you stand in our stead;[51] I believe and know that you will obtain for me and grant me that the bruised reed of my heart will not be entirely broken,[52] and that the smoldering wick of my faith[53] will not be extinguished. You do not sleep, my refuge; no, for he who watches over Israel will neither slumber nor sleep.[54] I know that you listen; get up, my God, and soothe the storms of my heart so that it will calm down, that I find the sweetness of your word and holy comfort, and that I learn to trust you with all my might:

I lay in strife and contestation,
    Help me, oh Lord Christ, in my weakness,
To your mercy alone I cling,
    You can make me stronger,
When temptation comes along / Ah, so fend it off,
    So that it will not knock me over / You can calm it down,
To keep all danger from me,
    I know that you will not let go,
    A M E N.

---

[48] Matthew 26; Luke 7; Matthew 15; Genesis 32.

[49] Genesis 32.

[50] Luke 22.

[51] 1st John 2.

[52] Hosea 42.

[53] Isaiah 42.

[54] Psalm 121.

The 7th Chapter.

Considers several beautiful contemplations in which the faithful heart will find comfort regarding the hideous image of the deceased body, the unfriendliness of the grave, and the gasping and twitching of the dying; so that at last the faithful heart will find refuge within the healing remedy of God and neither taste the bitterness nor feel the thorn of death.

I.

It is indeed manifest that a human will die.

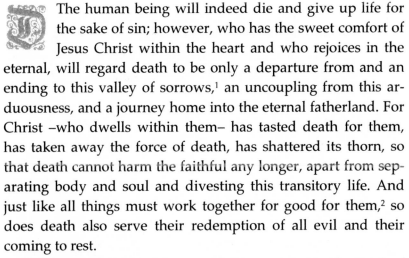 The human being will indeed die and give up life for the sake of sin; however, who has the sweet comfort of Jesus Christ within the heart and who rejoices in the eternal, will regard death to be only a departure from and an ending to this valley of sorrows,[1] an uncoupling from this arduousness, and a journey home into the eternal fatherland. For Christ –who dwells within them– has tasted death for them, has taken away the force of death, has shattered its thorn, so that death cannot harm the faithful any longer, apart from separating body and soul and divesting this transitory life. And just like all things must work together for good for them,[2] so does death also serve their redemption of all evil and their coming to rest.

Scripture witnesses this powerfully, as stated in the Book of Wisdom, THE SOULS OF THE RIGHTEOUS FALL INTO THE HANDS OF THE LORD;[3] and Christ himself says, I WILL COME BACK AND

---

[1] Philippians 1.
[2] Romans 8:28.
[3] Sirach 2:18.

TAKE YOU TO BE WITH ME THAT YOU MAY BE WHERE I AM.[4] Take notice and learn, dear soul, what your dying means: nothing more than a departure, a journey toward peace; to the faithful, dying is indeed nothing else than Lord Christ's arrival, and his taking the faithful to be with him.

LORD Jesus Christ, you eternal, essential light, enlighten my heart so that I –as a newly born human– will look at death with new eyes, and that I do not regard death to be my ruin, but only to be your messenger through which you claim me from this valley of sorrows and bring me to rest.

> Ah, do come, LORD Jesus, whenever you will,
> Uncouple, disperse, and bring home,
> Let your servant –who longs for your rest– fare in peace.
> A M E N.

II.
Death does make us abominable and hideous, cold and misshapen; we must grow stiff, and waste away in the grave.

This is also a punishment to which God exposes our bodies for the sake of our sins. The faithful children of God, however, do not look upon how hideously death mars us; they see through death and imagine how beautiful, renewed, delightful, blissful, pure, and glorious their bodies will be on that day; WHEN THE PERISHABLE HAS BEEN CLOTHED WITH THE IMPERISHABLE, AND THE MORTAL WITH IMMORTALITY; FOR THEN WILL BE FULFILLED THE WORD AS IT IS WRITTEN: DEATH HAS BEEN SWALLOWED UP IN VICTORY. DEATH, WHERE IS YOUR THORN? DEATH, WHERE IS YOUR VICTORY?[5]

Job comforted himself, when he was full of ulcers and boils, by commending himself to God, by carrying on throughout, and by saying, I KNOW THAT MY REDEEMER LIVES, AND THAT IN

---

[4] John 14:3.
[5] 1st Corinthians 15:54.

THE END HE WILL RAISE ME AGAIN FROM THE EARTH.[6] Oh, dear soul, how beautiful, how pure, how clean will our bodies be on that day; not a star in heaven will sparkle and glisten more beautifully –not even the sun and the moon– than our shining and shimmering bodies; when the LORD will transfigure our wasted bodies[7] and make them like his own transfigured body; indeed, when we will become not only like angels, but like the LORD himself.

Now we are our LORD God's kernel of wheat, which he sows in his graveyard; when the spring of God will dawn with the arrival of the right warmth and the rising of the right sun, however, then we will sprout and rise again, and we will bear righteous, eternal fruit. For it will be sown as perishable,[8] and it will be raised as imperishable; it will be sown in dishonor, and it will be raised in glory; it will be sown in weakness, and it will be raised in power; it will be sown a natural body, and it will be raised a spiritual body.

Strengthen me, my LORD Jesus Christ, so that I do not become frightened about the shapeless sight of the dead corpse, and that I do not become appalled when I think about my own body becoming a cold corpse, decaying in the grave, and turning into dust and earth; help me, instead, that I –in joyous hope– rather look upon the glory and purity which shall be revealed not only on my soul, but also on my body; grant me to delight in this wholeheartedly and to sing about it daily, saying:

---

[6] Job 19:25.

[7] Philippians 3.

[8] 1st Corinthians 15.

The kernel of wheat will bring no fruit,
   Unless it falls in the earth,
Thus must our earthly body,
   Became dust and ashes,
Before it reaches glory,
Which you, LORD Christ, have prepared for us,
   Through your passage to your father,
A M E N.

III.

Frightening things must be considered, the taste of which I dare not even imagine: death, dying, grave, tomb, being interred, being covered up, decaying, decomposing.

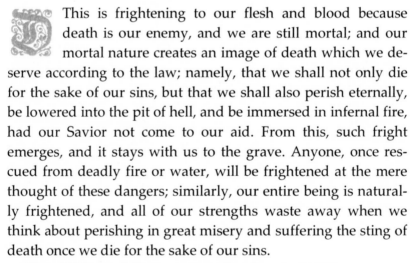 This is frightening to our flesh and blood because death is our enemy, and we are still mortal; and our mortal nature creates an image of death which we deserve according to the law; namely, that we shall not only die for the sake of our sins, but that we shall also perish eternally, be lowered into the pit of hell, and be immersed in infernal fire, had our Savior not come to our aid. From this, such fright emerges, and it stays with us to the grave. Anyone, once rescued from deadly fire or water, will be frightened at the mere thought of these dangers; similarly, our entire being is naturally frightened, and all of our strengths waste away when we think about perishing in great misery and suffering the sting of death once we die for the sake of our sins.

The children of God, on the other hand, shall learn a new language and see how the Holy Gospel speaks in it; for the gospel calls the death of the faithful a *sleep*, and the grave a *resting chamber*. Within the Gospel, Christ has not only borne the punishment of death for us, suffered the fright of hell for us, served the righteousness of God for us, and obtained life for us, the Holy Spirit has likewise repealed the dreadful notions of death and offered comfort to its faithful with another, a new

language. For this says the LORD, GO, MY PEOPLE, ENTER YOUR
ROOMS, AND SHUT THE DOOR BEHIND YOU; HIDE YOURSELVES FOR
A LITTLE WHILE UNTIL HIS WRATH HAS PASSED BY.[9] And also,
MANY WHO SLEEP UNDER THE EARTH WILL AWAKE.[10] And Christ
himself says, OUR FRIEND LAZARUS HAS FALLEN ASLEEP; BUT I
AM GOING THERE TO WAKE HIM UP.[11] And also, THE CHILD HAS
NOT DIED; INSTEAD, IT SLEEPS.[12] This is also said in the story of
the Passion, THE BODIES OF MANY HOLY PEOPLE WHO HAD SLEPT
WERE RAISED TO LIFE.[13]

Learn now, dear soul, to grasp this new language with renewed devotion; behold how the LORD – through his own
death – has transformed your dying into a gentle falling asleep,
and how he has turned your grave into a clean bed of rest.
When you die, you fall asleep; when you are laid into the
grave, you go to bed; when the grave is covered up, the door
behind you is closed; when your body wastes away, you rest
and keep sheltered until the wrath has passed you by.

Lord God, Holy Spirit, take my heart and fulfill it with the comforting
grace of my LORD Jesus Christ; teach me again to distinguish well
between the Laws and the Gospels; diminish in me the fright and the
dismay of death; and teach me your healing and comforting language
of the Gospels; grant me not only to hear it with my ears and to repeat
it with my mouth, but help me also to believe and to feel it wholeheartedly so that I –when my hour will come– do not die but fall
asleep gently; that I am laid not into the grave but into my chamber;
that I do not waste away but relax and rest until you will wake me up
again. Now I will lay myself into your arms, LORD Jesus, like a child
into the arms of its mother; I commend my soul to you, I fall asleep,
and I rest most comfortably:

---

[9] Isaiah 26: 20.

[10] Daniel 12:2.

[11] John 11:11b.

[12] Mark 5:39b.

[13] Matthew 27:51.

No one can awaken me,
Except you, LORD Jesus, Son of God,
You will open my grave hereafter,
And lead me to eternal life,
    A M E N.

IV.

I hear you say all this; but when I observe how humans die, I see them suffering, indeed; for several of them tremble, twitch, gasp, turn their eyes, sweat in fear.

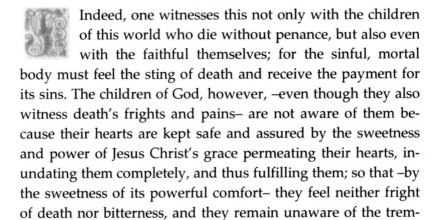 Indeed, one witnesses this not only with the children of this world who die without penance, but also even with the faithful themselves; for the sinful, mortal body must feel the sting of death and receive the payment for its sins. The children of God, however, –even though they also witness death's frights and pains– are not aware of them because their hearts are kept safe and assured by the sweetness and power of Jesus Christ's grace permeating their hearts, inundating them completely, and thus fulfilling them; so that –by the sweetness of its powerful comfort– they feel neither fright of death nor bitterness, and they remain unaware of the trembling and the sweat of fright. For the comfort of Jesus Christ is so great that it withstands anything and opposes all fright. And the name JESUS is so sweet that it repeals all bitterness, and that it provides a taste of the eternal blissfulness and salvation to the faithful even in the midst of death.

LORD Jesus Christ, you have tasted the bitterness of death for the sake of my sins; and you have sighed, trembled, and despaired for me in frights of your own death. I pray to you, safeguard me from a frightful and painful death; fulfill my heart with living faith and rich comfort, so that I will not fear death too much and not become too dismayed by its sting:

Oh, JESUS, by your sweet name,
In death, refresh this soul of mine,
A M E N.

V.

Is there no medicine which one may take
to have the sting of death be felt
and tasted less severely?

 Truly indeed, dear soul, for this says the LORD, your Savior, TRULY, TRULY I SAY TO YOU, WHOEVER OBEYS MY WORD WILL NEVER SEE DEATH.[14]

Listen, dear soul, to the words coming from the mouth of your heavenly doctor; make sure you learn well to take the medicine that can also drive away the pains of death; namely, the word of your LORD, Jesus Christ; not Moses' word which is the law of God; not the word of humans; not the word of sorcery or superstition; but the word of your Lord Christ; namely, the sermon of mercy of his Holy Gospel in which he proclaims promises and imparts to all faithful hearts the forgiveness of sin, righteousness in front of God, comfort of the Holy Spirit, and eternal life.

The Lord administers this word and this heavenly medicine to the faithful from his heart and from his mouth;[15] that is, the faithful hear it, retain it, keep it safe in a good-natured heart, adhere to it, rely on it in life and death; and, indeed, they seize it within their hearts with righteous, true, and strong faith; and within the word they taste Christ himself and his comfort; which spreads through them so that the taste of death's bitterness is replaced by the sweetness of Jesus Christ's word and comfort.

For Christ is within the word, and the word guides Christ and his power. Whoever wants to have the Lord shall have the word; and whoever has the word and retains it has the Lord

---

[14] John 8:51.
[15] Luke 8.

himself –including all the sweetness of his grace and of his comfort– will not see death; that is, he will neither feel death's bitterness and pain, nor perceive it, become aware of it, or taste it. For this is how the Lord himself explains it: TRULY I TELL YOU, he says, SOME WHO ARE STANDING HERE WILL NOT TASTE DEATH BEFORE THEY SEE THE SON OF MAN COMING IN HIS KING-DOM.[16] And he says also, I TELL YOU TRULY, SOME WHO ARE STANDING HERE WILL NOT TASTE DEATH BEFORE THEY SEE THE KINGDOM OF GOD.[17] That is, they build upon his trusted word, they rely on it, they taste Christ and his comfort within the word, they commend themselves to the true GOD with body and life, they rejoice, and they comfort themselves in their LORD Jesus Christ; they shroud themselves in the word like a dead body is shrouded in a death gown. And in doing so, everything stated in the word of Christ is indeed carried out for them, and they feel Christ and his grace including the taste of eternal life in their hearts.

Oh, you precious, beautiful, glorious, highly-praised medicine, which is assured and not deceiving. What else do you want, dear soul, and what else are you looking for? Take this heavenly medicine into your heart, use it well, and keep it safely with you every day and every moment. Behold, how the world boasts when it discovers medicine against fever, or against a toothache, or against sore eyes; how expensive and how valuable these medicines are; how much more shall you then boast about this heavenly, divine medicine of your Savior, which takes away even death, the father of all illnesses.

Do not question, dear soul, whether it is lasting and assured; you need only look at the examples of the saints who have used this medicine. Saint Stephen was full of faith and comforted in Jesus Christ; and that is why he passed blissfully, saying, LORD JESUS, RECEIVE MY SPIRIT.[18] Saint Paul also kept this

---

[16] Matthew 16:28.

[17] Luke 9:27.

[18] Acts 7:59.

heavenly medicine safely in his heart; that is why he was able to ward off death daily, saying, I DESIRE TO DEPART AND BE WITH CHRIST.[19]

Likewise did also the beloved martyrs: Saint Ignatius was fulfilled with the sweetness of the name Jesus Christ; and that is why he did not heed the torment. Saint Polycarp had been ignited by the love and desire of Jesus Christ; that is why he went into the fire comforted. Saint Laurent had the treasure of life within his heart, and he mocked his tyrant throughout all he his suffering; and when he saw that he was to be gruesomely tortured, he said: I HAD LONG WISHED FOR THIS RESTORATION. Saint Vincent felt the taste of eternal life in his faith; that is why –when being tormented in countless ways– he was full of joy, and he thanked God for deeming him worthy to suffer for the sake of Christ.

Likewise, Philip Melanchthon also testified that he, together with others, had heard and seen how the loyal man of God, Dr. Martin Luther –when laying deathly ill– spoke repeatedly this verse by Saint Paul to comfort his heart: FOR GOD HAS BOUND EVERYONE OVER TO DISOBEDIENCE SO THAT HE MAY HAVE MERCY ON THEM ALL.[20] Indeed, dear soul, these comforting verses of scripture restore our souls; they maintain the comfort within the heart; and the heart is restored through the power of the Holy Spirit until the end.

LORD Jesus Christ, you do have the word of eternal life[21] for which my soul yearns as it longs for your comfort. Indeed, my Savior, whoever retains your word and trusts in it has the rightful heavenly medicine –which does not deceive– against death and misery, and against all portals of hell. Oh, my LORD Jesus, fulfill my hungry heart with your word, and immerse me entirely in your comfort. Behold, my God, just like my dead body will be shrouded in a white veil and carried off, so do I wrap my soul into the word of your comforting prom-

---

[19] Philippians 1:23.
[20] Romans 11:32.
[21] John 6.

ise: your word is the truth and it will last forever;[22] that is why I will also be maintained eternally through the faith in your word. Indeed, my LORD Jesus, whoever believes in your word, believes also in you; whoever retains your word, retains you; whoever has you, also has life; whoever has life, cannot and will not taste death forever. For this you say, I AM THE RESURRECTION AND THE LIFE. WHOEVER BELIEVES IN ME WILL LIVE, EVEN THOUGH HE DIES; AND WHOEVER LIVES BY BELIEVING IN ME WILL NEVER DIE.[23] Do you believe this, my soul? Indeed, Lord Jesus! You know all things; you know that I believe in you, that I have you in my heart, that I find comfort in your word, that I completely depend on it; which is why I am certain that I am also among those who will not see death, who will not taste its bitterness, and who will not feel its sting. Bestow and impart that on me, Lord Christ, for the sake of your holy, righteous word. Amen!

---

[22] John 17; Isaiah 40.
[23] John 11:25.

The 8th Chapter.

Conveys many beautiful verses from Holy Scripture, as well
as several devotional prayers and lamentations, which
shall be recited for the dying person; this chapter
also conveys how the bystanders shall behave
who witness the departure and who have
given care to the deceased person.

I.

Do provide me now with several verses from Holy, Godly
Scripture, so that I become familiar with them, that
I find comfort in them at my end, and that
I may restore my soul.

Articles of Faith

Firstly, every Christian shall know well how to find
comfort in the Articles of Faith, which encompass the
entire sum of all teachings and verses of comfort. He
shall particularly meditate on the last three articles in which we
say, I BELIEVE IN THE FORGIVENESS OF SINS, IN THE RESURRECTION
OF THE FLESH, AND IN ETERNAL LIFE. And all articles shall be meticulously related to one's own faithful heart. Each heart shall
then espouse the articles and believe that everything will be
carried out to its benefit, and that comfort and salvation shall
be bestowed as assuredly as if it was the only one in this world
to receive and enjoy all these blessings.

Secondly, in order to affirm such faith, God has applied his
Holy Sacraments, and he has attached them as comforting seals
and symbols of grace to his articles of mercy. In them, everyone
can find lasting comfort in his Holy Baptism – within which he
has been accepted as a child of God, has entered an eternal, in-

dissoluble covenant of grace with his GOD, and has been cleansed and washed with the blood of Christ.

Thirdly, he also finds comfort in Holy Communion, where he –a child of God seated at the table of his Father– has been fed and restored; and where he now is assured of being a true limb of Christ with body and soul and an assured heir of all which Christ has attained by the sacrifice of his body and blood. Indeed, he is now assured that the Lord has lowered himself into his heart, that the Lord will strengthen him through the Holy Spirit at all times, that the Lord will maintain him steadfastly in faith, and that the Lord will be next to him with eternal comfort. Thereupon, the patient may either read several beautiful verses himself, or have them read to him; they are as follows:

> The woman's offspring will crush the head of the snake, and the snake will strike his heel.[1]
> The Son of God appeared to destroy the devil's work.[2]
> Eternal joy will be over their heads, joy and blissfulness will seize them, and pain and suffering must vanish.[3]
> Your dead will live; their bodies will rise; those who dwell under the earth, wake up and shout for joy.[4]
> Go, my people, enter your rooms, and shut the doors behind you; hide yourselves for a little while, until the wrath has passed by.[5]
> I came naked from my mother's womb, naked will I depart again; the Lord has given, the Lord has taken; praised be the name of the Lord.[6]

---

[1] Genesis 3:15.
[2] 1st John 3:8.
[3] Isaiah 35:10b.
[4] Isaiah 26:19a.
[5] Isaiah 26:20.
[6] Job 1:21b.

I know that my Redeemer lives, and he will in the end resurrect me from the earth; and I will afterwards be covered with my skin; and in my flesh I will see God; I myself will see him, behold him with my own eyes, and not a stranger.[7]

Is not Ephraim my dear son, and my beloved child? I still remember him, though I often spoke against him; therefore my heart yearns for him, so that I have great compassion for him, says the Lord.[8]

As surely as I live, says the Sovereign Lord, I take no pleasure in the death of the wicked, but rather that they turn from their ways and live.[9]

I will deliver them from hell; and I will rescue them from death; death, I will be a poison to you; hell, I will be a plague to you.[10]

As a deer gasps for fresh water, so, God! my soul gasps for you; my soul thirsts for God, for the living God; when will I get there, so that I can look upon God's face?[11]

Why are you downcast, my soul, and why are you so disturbed within me? Stand firm with God, for I will yet thank him, that he is my Savior and my God.[12]

When I only have you, I desire nothing in heaven and on earth: even if my body and soul may perish; you, God! are still my heart's comfort and my portion forever.[13]

The souls of the righteous are in God's hand, and no agony touches them: those without understanding regard them as if they had died; and their departure is regarded to be a torment, and their passing to be a ruin: now, however, they are at peace.[14]

---

[7] Jeremiah 19:25-27a.
[8] Jeremiah 31:20.
[9] Ezekiel 33:11b.
[10] Hosea 13:14a.
[11] Psalm 42:1-2.
[12] Psalm 42:5.
[13] Psalm 73:25-26.
[14] Wisdom 3:1-3.

We are the children of the righteous, and we hope for another
life, which God will give to those, who remain with him strongly and steadfastly in faith.[15]

Those who stand firm to the end, they will be saved.[16]

Come to me, all you who are troubled and burdened, I will refresh you.[17]

Look, this is the Lamb of God, which carries the world's sin.[18]

For God so loved the world that he gave his one and only son,
that whoever believes in him shall not perish, but have eternal
life.[19]

Very truly I say to you, whoever hears my word and believes him
who sent me, he has eternal life, and he will not be judged, but
has crossed over from death to life.[20]

I am the bread of life. Whoever comes to me will never go hungry, and whoever believes in me will never be thirsty.[21]

All those the Father gives me will come to me, and whoever
comes to me, I will not drive away.[22]

And this is the will of him who sent me, that I shall lose none of
those he has given me, but raise them up on the last day.[23]

Very truly, I say to you, whoever believes in me, he will have
eternal life.[24]

I am the light of the world; whoever follows me will never walk
in darkness, but he will have the light of life.[25]

Very truly, I say to you, whoever obeys my word, he will never
see death.[26]

---

[15] Tobit 13:13.

[16] Matthew 24:13.

[17] Matthew 11:28.

[18] John 1:29b.

[19] John 3:16.

[20] John 5:24.

[21] John 6:35b.

[22] John 6:37.

[23] John 6:39.

[24] John 6:47.

[25] John 8:12b.

My sheep hear my voice, and I know them, and they follow me, and I give them eternal life, and they will never perish, and no one can snatch them from my Father's hand. The Father, who has given them to me, is greater than everything, and no one can snatch them from my Father's hand; I and the Father are one.[27]

I am the resurrection and the life; whoever believes in me, he will live, even when he dies; and whoever lives and believes in me, he will never die.[28]

My Father's house has many rooms; if that were not so, would I have told you: I am going there to prepare a place for you; and if I go and prepare a place for you, I will come back and take you to be with me, so that you will be where I am.[29]

I am the way, the truth, and the life; no one comes to the Father, except through me.[30]

Now this is eternal life, that they know you, the only true God, and whom you have sent, Jesus Christ.[31]

Father! I wish that wherever I am, those whom you have given to me will also be with me, so that they will see my glory, which you have given to me; for you have loved me before the world has been created.[32]

There is no other salvation, there is also no other name given to us humans, wherein we shall be saved.[33]

All the prophets testify about [the Lord Jesus], that everyone who believes in him, shall receive the forgiveness of sins.[34]

Where the sin has become powerful, grace has become even more powerful.[35]

---

[26] John 8:51.
[27] John 10:27-30.
[28] John 11:25b-26a.
[29] John 14:2-3.
[30] John 14:6b.
[31] John 17:3.
[32] John 17:24.
[33] Acts 4:12.
[34] Acts 10:43.

If God is for us, who can be against us? He who did not spare even his own son, but who gave him up for all of us: how shall he not, along with him, give us everything? Who would accuse the ones chosen by God? It is God, who makes righteous. Who would condemn? Christ is the one, who has died; and indeed much more, who was raised to life, who is at the right hand of God, and who stands in for us.[36]

I am certain that neither death nor life, nor any other creature is able to separate me from the love of God [. . .] that is in Christ Jesus, our Lord.[37]

God has bound everyone over to disobedience, so that he may have mercy with us all.[38]

For none of us lives for ourselves, and none of us dies for ourselves; if we live, we live for the Lord; and if we die, we die for the Lord; therefore, whether we live or die, we belong to the Lord.[39]

For as in Adam all will die, thus in Christ all will be made alive.[40]

For we know, once our earthly hut in which we live is destroyed, that we have a building constructed by God; a house, that is not built by hands, but which is eternal in heaven.[41]

God is faithful; he will not let you be tempted beyond what you can bear; but he will provide a way out of temptation, so that you can endure it.[42]

That Christ alone will be exalted in my body, whether in life or in death. For Christ is my life, and to die is my gain. If I am to go on living in the body, I will labor more fruitfully, yet I do not know, which I should choose; for I am torn between the two. I

---

[35] Romans 5:20b.

[36] Romans 8:31-34.

[37] Romans 8:38-39.

[38] Romans 11:32.

[39] Romans 14:7-8.

[40] 1st Corinthians 15:22.

[41] 2nd Corinthians 5:1.

[42] 1st Corinthians 10:13b.

desire to depart and be with Christ, for that would be far better.[43]

Our citizenship is in heaven, where we will also await the Savior Jesus Christ, the Lord, who will transfigure our trivial body, so that it will become like his transfigured body.[44]

This is undeniably true, and it is a trustworthy, precious word, that Christ Jesus has come into the world, to save the sinners, among whom I am the most distinguished.[45]

The time of my departure is at hand; I have fought a good fight; I have finished the race; I have kept faith; henceforth, the crown of righteousness is in store for me, which the Lord, the righteous judge, will give to me on that day; however, not to me alone, but also to all, who love his appearance.[46]

Fight the good fight of faith, take hold of the eternal life to which you were called.[47]

I know in whom I believe; I know and I am confident, that he will keep my deposit in store, until that day.[48]

Keep in mind Jesus Christ; he has arisen from the dead.[49]

By God's power, you will be brought to salvation through faith.[50]

The blood of Jesus Christ, the Son of God, cleanses us from all sins.[51]

This is how God showed his love for us: GOD sent his one and only son into the world, that we may live through him.[52]

Within this, love is manifest: not that we loved God, but that he loved us, and that he sent his son for the forgiveness of our sins.[53]

---

[43] Philippians 1:20b-23.

[44] Philippians 3:20-21.

[45] 1st Timothy 1:15.

[46] 2nd Timothy 4:6b-8.

[47] 1st Timothy 6:12a.

[48] 2nd Timothy 1:12b.

[49] 2nd Timothy 2:8a.

[50] 1st Peter 1:5b.

[51] 1st John 1:7b.

[52] 1st John 4:9.

Here we do not have an enduring city, but we are looking for the city that is to come.[54]

Whoever I love, those I punish and chastise.[55]

Be faithful until death, then I will give you the crown of life.[56]

Whoever overcomes, to him I will grant to sit with me on my chair; just as I have overcome, and have sat with my Father on his chair.[57]

They have overcome through the blood of the lamb, and through the word of their witness; and they have not loved their life until death.[58]

Blessed are the dead, who die in the name of the Lord from now on.[59]

From these and from other verses of comfort, dear soul, choose several which comfort you most pleasingly; become as familiar with them as with the Holy Lord's Prayer; prepare them as you would prepare provisions of your own death a few years in advance, and keep them safely until needed for shrouding the body. Likewise, choose several verses for yourself, and learn to understand them well and to store them safely, so that you can wrap your soul into them during your end. For then, the mind often becomes weak, the memory decreases, long sermons may no longer be comprehensible, little attention is paid to elevated words in flowery oratories; instead, a verse of comfort or a word of comfort –coming from the mouth of God–[60] will delight, refresh, nourish, and restore heart, body, and soul. Learning this only at the deathbed, however, may turn out to be difficult and sometimes even too late.

---

[53] 1st John 4:9-10.

[54] Hebrews 13:14.

[55] Revelation 3:19a.

[56] Revelation 2:10b.

[57] Revelation 3:21.

[58] Revelation 12:11.

[59] Revelation 14:13b.

[60] Deuteronomy 8; Matthew 4.

LORD Jesus Christ! open my heart through your Holy Spirit, so that I delight in hearing the verses of your holy words, that I keep them well in mind, that I repeat them often, and that I may enrich my heart with them. Grant me to keep your word and not to become like a leaky vessel that does not retain any lessons.[61] Open my understanding, strengthen my memory, and remind me of your comfort without ceasing! Help me to retain your word within a good heart and patiently to bring forth the fruit for eternal salvation.[62] Amen.

II.

Teach me also several short prayers which will restore me on my deathbed, and which I may recite also to others who are dying.

 I have already presented many beautiful short prayers to you that may be of good use. Now I want to present additional prayers to you that have been composed by other inspired authors.

I.

The first and most distinguished prayer is the beloved Lord's Prayer, which the Lord himself has taught to us; it encompasses, in striking brevity, all of our afflictions concerning and burdening us – in life as well as in death. When you wish to pray, says the Lord, you shall say this:[63]

Our Father, who is in heaven, hallowed be your name. Your kingdom come. Your will be done, as in heaven, so also on earth. Our daily bread give us today. And forgive us our debts, as we forgive our debtors. And lead us not into temptation, but

---

[61] Sirach 21:14.
[62] Luke 8:14b.
[63] Matthew 6:9a.

deliver us from evil.[64] For yours is the kingdom, the power, and the glory, in eternity. Amen.

II.

Oh LORD God! in my affliction,
  I call on you, that you help me;
  I commend my body and soul
  Into your hands: send me your angel,
  Who will protect me, when I depart
  From this world, whenever it pleases you.
LORD Jesus Christ! you have died
  on the cross, you Lamb of God!
  Your wounds bleeding, in utter anguish,
  Your precious blood awards my benefit,
  Your suffering and dying makes me the heir
  To your kingdom, just like the angels,
  That I will live with you forever.
Oh Holy Spirit! You are my comforter;
  At my end, send me your comfort;
  Do not leave me when I am assailed
  By the devil's power, by the stature of death.
  Oh Lord, my shelter, according to your word,
  Give to me eternal life.
  A M E N.

III.

Help me, Savior, help me in fright and affliction,
Have mercy on me, you loyal God,
I am indeed your beloved child;
In spite of the world, the devil, and all sin,
I trust in you, my God and Lord.
When I have you, what more do I need;
I do have you, LORD Jesus Christ,
You are my God and my Redeemer,

---

[64] Matthew 6:9b-13.

Therein my heart rejoices;
I am of good courage and I await you,
I have complete faith on your name;
Help me, Savior, help me, that I say Amen.

IV.

Oh LORD be my refuge,
Even when my mouth will utter words no more,
And even when my ears will hear no longer,
Through your spirit, do instruct me.
LORD, you are my rock, my strength and comfort,
When death knocks at my heart,
Through which my eyes may turn away,
Oh stand by me and help me at my end.
LORD, to you I commend my spirit,
Your gracious sight, turn it toward me,
By means of your bitter suffering and death,
Do not let me perish in any sin
Worsened by my enemy.
Oh Lord, tear me from his jaws,
And instill in me your comforting word;
I plead for your reconciliation.
Let my conscience also feel,
That I am cleansed from all sin.
Oh faithful God, I plead wholeheartedly,
Give me patience in my pain,
Through Jesus Christ hear my prayer,
Let your servant die in peace.
Rescue me from affliction and agony,
Accompany my soul into the halls of heaven
Into your realm guided by your angel,
So that I will live with you eternally, Amen.

V.

Being a poor sinner, I am nothing,
Only in God's son lies my gain,

His becoming human is my comfort,
  He has rescued me through his blood.
Oh God, Father, govern me
  Steadfastly with your spirit,
Let your son, my comfort and my life,
  Always soar in my heart.
And when the hour is at hand,
  Take me to you, LORD Jesus Christ.
For I am yours, and you are mine,
  How eagerly I want to be with you.
LORD Jesus Christ, help me,
  So that I remain a tiny limb in you,
And that I hereafter rise again with you,
  To enter into your glory,
Into your kingdom with your angels,
  To laud and praise you eternally, Amen.

VI.

Lord Jesus Christ, you loyal refuge,
You Son of God, and you eternal word;
My comfort, my salvation, and my true joy
In my fright and great suffering;
My steady fortress and assurance,
My strength, my power, light of my life;
Great is your mercy and your benevolence,
Without boundary is your love in eternity
Through your great kindheartedness;
My grieving heart is always restored.
My sin upsets me night and day,
Oh comfort me so that I will not despair.
Spray me, Lord, and make me pure
With the rose-colored blood of yours,
Rescue me from eternal death;
By your holy, red wounds,
Let my heart feel the angelic joy,
Which lasts and remains in eternity, Amen.

VII.

LORD Jesus Christ, true human and true God,
Who did suffer torture, fright and scorn,
Who in the end died for me on the cross,
And won your Father's grace toward me;
By your bitter suffering I plead,
That you be merciful toward me, a sinner,
As I arrive at death's affliction now,
And as I am wrestling with death,
As all my awareness will vanish,
And my ears will no longer hear,
And my tongue will utter nothing any longer,
And when my heart will break of fright,
When my mind will understand no more,
And all my human aid will melt away,
Then, oh LORD Christ, swiftly come to me,
Help me in my final moment,
And lead me out of the valley of sorrows;
Shorten also the pains of death,
Drive away the evil spirits,
Stay with me unfailingly in spirit
Until the soul departs from the body;
Take my soul, LORD, into your hands,
The body will find its rest within the earth,
Until the day of judgment will approach;
Grant me a joyous rising,
At the last judgment, be my spokesperson,
And do not keep in mind my sin,
Out of grace, grant me life,
As you have promised me;
In your word, in that I trust.
Truly, truly I say to you,
Whoever keeps my word and believes in me,
Will not be condemned,
And will not taste death eternally;
And even when he dies here on earth,

He will certainly not perish,
But he will, by a strong hand,
Be torn free from the bonds of death,
And taken to me into my realm,
And there he shall, together with me,
Live in joy eternally;
For that, LORD, help us mercifully.
Oh LORD, forgive us all our debt,
Grant that we will wait patiently
Until our hour is at hand,
Grant our faith to remain always strong,
And to believe steadfastly in your word,
Until we pass away blessedly, Amen.

VIII.

Lord Jesus Christ, into your hand,
I commend my final moment;
My soul, take it to you,
And lead it to your Father.
It is covered with your blood,
This is indeed my greatest gift.
I die, and now I want to be with you,
Without all sorrow, without all pain.
My life is nothing here on earth,
Even if it lasts for many years.
LORD, help me keep this in mind,
When I repose into your mercy.
I trust and I believe through Jesus Christ,
That you, oh God, will be merciful with me, Amen.

IX.

Oh Jesus, little lamb of God,
Whether I live or die, I am yours.
I pray, let me be, together with you,
An heir of your kingdom.
For whom else did you suffer afflictions of death?

So many welts and bloody wounds?
If I shall not receive
The blessedness in eternity?
Why have you given up and locked into the grave
Your body and your life?
If not so that your death shall
Chase away my death, you loyal God?
Therefore, oh Jesus, stand by me,
Impart your unfailing comfort and benefit.
Do not abandon me, LORD Jesus Christ,
For I have been cleansed by your blood.
Peacefully let me go to sleep,
And let me find quiet calm in you.
Let me see your face, LORD,
Grant me a blessed ending.
This I plead by the suffering of yours,
Let this be my last wish;
Then I will always praise
You, oh Lord God, in eternity, Amen.

X.

Here I lie, a wretched creature,
Can move neither hands nor legs.
Of fright my heart bursts inside me,
My life is wrestling with death.
My mind and all my senses are dull,
Of life I am tired and sick.
My hearing and my sight are gone,
Dying blessedly is my gain.
Therefore, Lord Christ, rush to my aid,
Ward off the devil's fiery arrows.
Now he roars all around me,
Like a lion and a ferocious bear.
So that nothing will separate me from your love,
No contestation, nor fright or woe.
In your kingdom let me become

The least of your servants.
Bestow on me a steadfast faith,
So that I will be just and blessed.
Won by your precious blood
From sin, from death and burning hell.
If now my hour shall draw near,
So let your angels stand around me.
From the valley of sorrows may they lead
My soul into the halls of heaven.
So that I, together with all your saints,
Within the choir of the dear angels,
Praise your holy name,
In all eternity, Amen.

XI.

Oh God, how much heartache
  I encounter at this time.
  The narrow path is filled with tribulation
  On which I shall walk toward heaven.
  How hard it is for flesh and blood
  To be compelled to eternal benevolence.
To whom shall I turn?
  Toward you, Lord Jesus, that is my intent.
  My heart has found comfort, aid and counsel
  Always and assuredly with you.
  Nobody has ever been abandoned,
  Who has trusted in Jesus Christ.
You are the great miraculous man,
  Shown by your deeds and through your person.
  What miracle it is to know
  That you, my God, have been born a human,
  And that you lead us, through your death,
  Wholly and miraculously out of all affliction!
Jesus, my LORD and God alone,
  How sweet your name is to me,
  No grief is too severe,

To bring even more joy through your sweet name.
No misery is too bitter
To find relief through your sweet comfort.
Even when my body and soul waste away,
Then you know, Lord, that I don't mind,
As long as I have you, then I retain,
What shall bring eternal joy to me.
I am yours indeed with body and with soul,
How can sin, death, and hell threaten me?
No better faith is here on earth,
Than with you, Lord Jesus Christ.
I know that you will not leave me;
Your truth will remain firm eternally,
You are my righteous, faithful shepherd,
Who will forever watch over me.
Jesus, my joy, my honor, my fame,
My heart's treasure and my fortune;
I cannot even fathom,
How much joy your name can bring.
Whoever has faith and love within the heart,
Will be made aware with this deed.
That is why I have said it many times,
If I would not rejoice in you,
Then I would rather wish to die,
And even wish that I had never been born.
For whoever does not have you within the heart,
Is dead already when still alive.
Jesus, you noble, worthy bridegroom,
My most precious adornment on this earth,
In you alone I find delight,
Far more than in all golden treasure.
As often as I only think of you,
My spirit, heart, and mind rejoice.
When I place my hope in you,
Then I feel peace and comfort within me.
When I pray and sing in need,

Then my heart becomes wholly pleased,
  Your spirit affirms that this is indeed
  The foretaste of eternal life.
Therefore will I, since I still live,
  Carry my cross eagerly after you;
  My God, do prepare me for that,
  So that I always serve you well.
  Help me to grasp my matters rightfully,
  So that I can complete my course.
Help me also to compel my flesh and blood,
  To beware of sin and shame,
  Maintain my heart purely in faith,
  Then I will live and die for you alone.
  Jesus, my comfort, hear my plea,
  Oh my Savior, if only I were with you,
  A M E N.

These and similar prayers shall be well practiced daily – to commend oneself to God and to plead for a blessed hour of death.

These include also:

The 6ᵗʰ Psalm: Oh Lord, do not rebuke me in your anger, etc.
The 23ʳᵈ Psalm: The LORD is my shepherd, etc.
The 25ᵗʰ Psalm: In you, LORD my God, I put my trust, etc.
The 32ⁿᵈ Psalm: Blessed is the one whose transgressions are for-
  given, etc.
The 42ⁿᵈ Psalm: As the deer pants, etc.
The 51ˢᵗ Psalm: Have mercy on me, oh God, etc.

III.

Some patients also like to hear songs: which of them shall be sung to them?

 It is known that beautiful songs —when sung with devotion— may take much sadness and grief away from the heart; furthermore, singing may also provide plentiful and beautiful comfort, so that the hearts of the dying may become cheerful and encouraged; they are then reminded of the heavenly music of angels —praising God in eternal joy— which we may help provide to them. One should, nevertheless, follow the patient's wishes, and sing what is desired; among them:

1. We all believe in one God, etc.[65]
2. Our Father in the heavenly kingdom, etc.[66]
3. With peace and joy I follow my course, etc.[67]
4. From deep affliction I cry out to you, etc.[68]
5. Now we pray to the Holy Spirit, etc.[69]
6. Have mercy on me, oh Lord God, etc.[70]
7. God, Father, stay with us, etc.[71]
8. In the midst of life we are with death, etc.[72]

---

[65] *Wir glauben all an einen Gott,* text: Martin Luther (1524), melody: Wittenberg (15th century).

[66] *Vater unser im Himmelreich,* text: Martin Luther (1539), melody: Salzburg (14th century).

[67] *Mit Fried und Freud ich fahr dahin,* text and melody: Martin Luther, (1524).

[68] *Aus tiefer Not schrei ich zu dir,* text und 1st melody: Martin Luther (1524), 2nd melody: Wolfgang Dachstein (1524).

[69] *Nun bitten wir den Heiligen Geist,* text: 13th century and Martin Luther (1524), melody: Jistebnitz (13th century).

[70] *Erbarm dich mein, O Herre Gott,* text: Erhard Hegenwalt (1524).

[71] *Gott der Vater steh uns bei,* text: Martin Luther (1524) after a German litany, 15th century, melody: Halberstadt (ca. 1500).

9. Oh dear Christian, be comforted, etc.[73]

10. Now let us bury the body, etc.[74]

11. I call on you, LORD Jesus Christ, etc.[75]

12. To you alone, LORD Jesus Christ, etc.[76]

13. Through Adam's fall, etc.[77]

14. Salvation has come to us, etc.[78]

15. When the hour is at hand, etc.[79]

These and other songs can be found in the hymn book. One can also find seasonal songs for Christmas, Easter, or Pentecost, and sing them according to wishes of the ill person.

---

[72] *Mitten wir im Leben sind,* text: Salzburg (1456) after the antiphon "Media vita morte sumus", 11ᵗʰ century and Martin Luther (1524), melody: Salzburg (1456) / Johann Walter (1524).

[73] *Ach, lieben Christen, seid getrost,* text Johannes Gigas (1561).

[74] *Nun legen wir den Leib ins Grab,* text: Michael Weiße (1531) and Martin Luther (1540).

[75] *Ich ruf zu dir, Herr Jesu Christ,* text: probably Johannes Agricola (1526/1527), melody: Hagenau (1526/1527).

[76] *Allein zu dir, Herr Jesu Christ,* text: Konrad Hubert, (before 1540), melody: Paul Hofhaimer (1512).

[77] *Durch Adams Fall ist ganz verderbt,* text: Lazarus Spengler, melody: Wittenberg (1529).

[78] *Es ist das Heil uns kommen her,* text: Paul Speratus (1523), melody: Mainz (around 1390), Nürnberg (1523/1524).

[79] *Wenn mein Stündlein vorhanden ist,* text: Nikolaus Herman (1562) and Köln (1574), melody: Frankfurt am Main (1569) / Tübingen (1591).

IV.

Do also provide me with some short lamentations which may be applied when the ill person is very weak, has light breath, cannot speak; particularly such verses which commend his soul to God.

I.

LORD, now you let your servant journey onward in peace, as you have promised, for my eyes have seen your Savior.[80]

II.

Father, into your hands I commend my spirit.[81]

III.

Into your hands I commit my spirit; deliver me, LORD, my faithful God.[82]

IV.

LORD Jesus, receive my spirit.[83]

V.

Ah, you sweet Jesus Christ, since you have been born a man, safeguard me from hell.

VI.

Lord, stay with us, for it will be evening soon, and the day is spent.[84]

---

[80] Luke 2:29-30.
[81] Luke 23:26.
[82] Psalm 31:5.
[83] Acts 7:59.
[84] Luke 24:29.

VII.

Oh, stay with us, LORD Jesus Christ, since the evening is at
  hand; your work, oh Lord, the eternal light, let it not extinguish
  for us.

VIII.

I would like to depart and be with Christ.[85]

IX.

Oh you my dearest Jesus,
  Make yourself a clean, soft bed,
  To rest within my heart's shrine,
  That I will never forget you.

X.

Worthy am I not, and I am sorry,
  I confess my sins, I readily search for mercy,
  I, an unworthy servant, believe in Christ,
  His blood alone will make me just.

XI.

Deliver us from all evil,
  These times and days are wretched,
  Deliver us from eternal death,
  And rescue us in our last affliction,
  Bestow on us, LORD, a blessed end,
  Take our soul into your hands.
Amen, which means, may this come true,
  Strengthen our faith for evermore,
  Help that we do not doubt,
  For which we have prayed,
  Upon your word and in your name,
  We do give voice to the *Amen*.

---

[85] Philippians 1:23.

XII.

Jesus, the sweet name of yours,
    Restores my soul even in death.

XIII.

This soul which you have redeemed,
    Bestow your comfort on it, LORD Jesus.

XIV.

LORD Jesus Christ, my comfort and joy,
    I wait for you at all times,
    Come whenever you will,
    I am ready.

XV.

Come, LORD Christ, come, you loyal God,
    And bring an end to me,
    Defeat the last enemy, death,
    And lead me out of misery.
    Bring me to the righteous Fatherland,
    Since you have applied your blood for me,
    Let me journey home in peace.

XVI.

A heart soaked with remorse and sorrow,
    Covered with Christ's precious blood,
    It sighs to God with true faith,
    Like a cooing dove;
    At last, it will be rightfully comforted,
    And rescued from all fright and need.
    Therefore, believe, pray, hope, and be patient,
    So that God in heaven will be kind;
    You will praise his benevolence,
    In his church and great congregation, Amen.

XVII.

God, the eternal Father's benevolence,
 The LORD Jesus' precious blood,
 The Holy Spirit's comfort and courage,
 Shall become my eternal inheritance.

XVIII.

LORD Jesus, come swiftly,
 Give me a blessed end,
 Receive my soul into your hands,
 A M E N.

V.

What shall the bystanders do when they see that a Christian has bid farewell, has been comforted until the end, and has passed away blessedly?

Sighing and weeping is not to be held against anyone, for it is natural. Be wary, however, of heathen sighing, of boisterous crying,[86] and of other misconduct; for we are Christians, and we shall let ourselves be comforted as those who have faith and who have strong, firm, indubitable hope that our dead have not died, but have passed on; that they are not lost, but delivered from all evil and taken home by the LORD. We do not believe in thousands of possible reincarnations and in a return back to this misery.

That is why we shall rather thank God for such a blessed departure; and we shall learn how to live in a Christian manner and how to die blessedly as it is written, REMEMBER YOUR SAINTS AND FAITHFUL, WHO SPOKE THE WORD OF GOD TO YOU. CONSIDER THE OUTCOME OF THEIR WAY OF LIFE AND IMITATE THEIR FAITH.[87] Indeed, we shall fall on our knees and pray:

---

[86] 1st Thessalonians 4.
[87] Hebrews 13:7.

We thank you, LORD Jesus Christ, eternal prince of life, that you have steadfastly maintained this dear human being in true penance and faith, and that you have granted a blessed end. Oh, how lovingly the soul is now being carried toward heaven; how well the soul now feels. For it is said of Lazarus' soul, who died in front of the rich man's door, HIS SOUL WAS CARRIED BY THE ANGELS INTO ABRAHAM'S LAP.[88] Therefore, I have faith and I know for certain, even though I cannot see with my mortal, bodily, dark eyes the presence of the many holy angels who, surrounding the bed, have waited for this soul. Now it will be taken home; now it enters into eternal paradise. Now it rests in the arms of Lord Jesus and on his lap. Now all its grief has come to an end; now the LORD will wipe away all tears from its eyes,[89] and he will bestow on it eternal peace and comfort, with eternal joy and bliss. Eternal joy will be upon your head; bliss and joy will seize you, but fright and sadness will be far from you. Oh, you dear soul, how well you are now; you have carried the yoke of Christ; you have died; and now you live.

Oh, LORD Jesus Christ, have mercy also on us who still live here and who are left behind; comfort us in this valley of sorrow, and help us bear this troublesome misery with patience until the end. Grant us also that we follow with such faith, that we stand ready daily and hourly, and that we also –like this beloved person– come to a blessed end of our work, and that we may journey onward with peace and joy,

A M E N.

---

[88] Luke 16:22.
[89] Acts 21.

The 9th Chapter.

Describes where the immortal souls will arrive after their departure and in which condition. It also contemplates the resurrection of our bodies, the joy of eternal bliss, and the pain of eternal damnation.

I.

Since the souls are immortal, where will they go, and how will they fare when they depart from the bodies?

Scripture tells us of thereof –beautifully and comfortingly– in the following verses:

> Do not be afraid of those who kill the body but cannot kill the soul. Rather be afraid of the one who can destroy body and soul in hell.[1]
>
> The dust shall return to the earth as it was, and the spirit shall return to God who gave it.[2]
>
> I desire to depart and be with Christ, which is better by far.[3]
>
> The penitent evildoer, when he gave up his spirit, spoke to the LORD: Lord, remember me when you come into your kingdom. And Jesus said to him: Truly, I tell you, today you will be with me in paradise.[4]
>
> The souls of the just are in God's hands, and no torment shall touch them; the ignorant will see them as dead, and their departure will be regarded as painful, and their passing away as perishing; however, they will be in peace.[5]

---

[1] Matthew 10:28.

[2] Ecclesiastes 12:7.

[3] Philippians 1:23.

[4] Luke 23:42-43.

[5] Sirach 3:1-3.

The just person, even when he dies too early, will nevertheless be in peace.[6]

Comfort, comfort my people, says your God.[7]

The time came when the beggar died and the angels carried him to Abraham's side. ... but now he is comforted here, and you are in agony.[8]

My Father's house has many rooms; if that were not so, would I have told you that I am going there to prepare a place for you? And if I go and prepare a place for you, I will come back and take you to be with me that you are where I am.[9]

For we know that if the earthly house we live in is destroyed, we have a building from God, a house not made with hands, that stands eternal in heaven.[10]

We are confident and would prefer to be away from the body and at home with the LORD.[11]

You will see me; because I live, you shall also live.[12]

Seek that which is above, not that which is on earth.[13]

For the Jerusalem which is above is freedom and mother of us all.[14]

You make known to me the path of life; you fill me with joy and eternal pleasures at your right hand.[15]

Behold, dear soul, these wonderful and most comforting verses spoken by God assure us that human souls are quite unlike human bodies; for they are spirits, like angels, and they will never die. And when the souls of the righteous depart from their bodies, the holy angels will receive and carry them to

---

[6] Sirach 4:7.

[7] Isaiah 40:1.

[8] Luke 16:22 and 25.

[9] John 14:2-3.

[10] 2ⁿᵈ Corinthians 5:1.

[11] 2ⁿᵈ Corinthians 5:8.

[12] John 14:19.

[13] Colossians 3:2.

[14] Galatians 4:31.

[15] Psalm 16:11.

God, and they will be at home with the LORD, with Christ; and they will live in paradise, in heaven above; and they will soar in honor and in delight beyond words; they will be endearingly comforted in pureness and in glory; they will be quiet, peaceful, and in God's hand – without affliction, fright, grief, or want. Once the souls depart from the bodies, and they will be free and thrive more effectively without the body than before; for the body in this life is more cumbersome and obstructive for the souls. In their mortal, wretched bodies here on earth, the souls praise, call on, serve, rejoice, and find comfort in God as well as delight in all his works; outside the bodies, however they will carry out such things much more gloriously, for they will be entirely without sin, without weakness, and without obstruction. Fathom, dear soul, how beautiful and comforting this will be; who could possibly be frightened of death?

The souls of the unbelieving, on the other hand, will swiftly end up within the devil's power, and they will be carried off to the place of agony, as is witnessed by the soul of the rich man;[16] there the souls are in unrest, in discord, in fright, in affliction, in lament and woes, without any comfort and mercy, in filth and darkness, in relentless weeping and gnashing of teeth, until the day of judgment; then their sorrow and misery will increase even more and not end eternally.

LORD Jesus Christ, my comfort and my blissfulness, how my soul yearns for you; indeed, as the deer pants for fresh water,[17] so does my soul also cry out for you. My soul thirsts after you, my living God. Oh, when will I get to the place where I shall behold your sight? Oh, how tired and exasperated I am of this arduous valley of sorrows wherein I labor for you, my God, wherein I serve your congregation. I shall claim, together with dear Paul: I DESIRE TO DEPART AND BE WITH MY LORD CHRIST, WHICH IS BETTER BY FAR; BUT IT IS MORE NECESSARY THAT I LIVE IN THE BODY AND BRING FRUIT. I DO NOT KNOW WHAT I

---

[16] Luke 16.
[17] Psalms 42.

SHALL CHOOSE.[18] Lord Jesus, you eternal wisdom, you know my time, and my days remain in your hands. Release me, my LORD, whenever you wish; my heart longs for rest; indeed, for rest that is living eternally; from darkness to light; from grief to joy; from unrest to peace; from hardship to glory; from weakness to perfection. Lord Jesus, you know all things; you know also that my soul loves you wholeheartedly, and that it bears a passionate longing to behold your sight. Look, dearest Savior, how the tears of love flow from my eyes. Understand, that my eyes weep of joy, and that my heart is sick, yearning, thirsting, longing for love, and that it wishes to be at home with you, resting in your lap within your arms. My Lord and my God, how well I will feel there; my soul will cry out with great joy, saying: IT IS GOOD TO BE HERE; IT IS GOOD TO BE HERE.[19] Lord Jesus, remember me in your kingdom and speak to my soul: TODAY YOU WILL BE WITH ME IN PARADISE.[20] Amen.

II.

Will the dear souls –since they know that their remains decay so pitifully in the cold earth– yearn for their bodies; and will time seem long to them since the day of judgment and the resurrection of the body will be drawn out?

I must confess that such thoughts often sadden me. However, one must firstly know that after their departure our souls are with Christ, and that they soar in pureness and glory, so that they will also have much higher understanding and wisdom, recognizing more clearly the wonderfully righteous counsel and will of God; and therefore they will know for certain that no hardship will afflict their bodies, but that they will rest gently and quietly, and that every particle and crumb of their bones will be kept safe by the al-

---

[18] Philippians 1:22-24.
[19] Matthew 17:4.
[20] Luke 23:43.

mightiness of God, so that no one will perish until the resurrection is at hand.

Secondly, the dear blessed souls will be at such a place, and in such joy, where there cannot be unrestrained, gloomy desire or yearning. For even if they continue to remember their bodies and long for the judgment of God –as described in the Revelation of John–,[21] such remembrance and yearning will not sadden them, but belong to their blissfulness in which they will soar for the glory and praise of God to whom they give honor and whose will they let reign.

The children of God –in this miserable life when they still dwell in their human bodies– long for the final redemption and yearn for the future with Christ; and whoever does not long for it, certainly does not love the Lord Jesus. Should the dear souls with Christ not wish for all sinfulness in the world finally to end, and for eternal perfection to commence? Such desire and yearning cannot possibly cause them grief, sadness, or painful longing; for they are with God, the LORD, beyond this world, where there is no time, no distinction between years and days; and when there is no time, neither burdensome longing nor yearning can exist. For thus says scripture, A THOUSAND YEARS IN YOUR SIGHT ARE LIKE A DAY THAT PAST YESTERDAY, OR LIKE A WATCH IN THE NIGHT.[22] And also, BUT DO NOT FORGET ONE THING, DEAR FRIENDS: WITH THE LORD A DAY IS LIKE A THOUSAND YEARS, AND A THOUSAND YEARS ARE LIKE A DAY.[23]

That is why, dear soul, cease having such thoughts and surrender yourself into the hand of the LORD, who is your creator, your GOD, your comfort, your rest, your shield, and your complete satisfaction, both now and after this life, and then in all eternity.

---

[21] Revelation 6.

[22] Psalm 90:4.

[23] 2nd Peter 3:8.

LORD Jesus Christ, you see and you know that I love your presence wholeheartedly,[24] and I ask you with all my strength that when you arrive, you will destroy the ungodly, sinful ways of the world, that you exercise your righteous judgment on the devil and on all our enemies, and that you will let commence eternal joyousness when you shall be everything in every part.[25] Indeed, my Lord Jesus, all other creatures are fearful, and they long for –as Saint Paul says–[26] liberation from futility to which they are subjected by hope; shall we, the children of God, not long for our final redemption? Is it your holy will, LORD Jesus, and have you decided in your counsel that I shall witness your joyful arrival? So have it done, my LORD, and my Redeemer; oh, how I will listen to your trumpets sounding great joy, and how I will come toward you in great leaps through the air. If you, however, let me depart before that time, and if you take my soul to you into the joyful paradise, then I say: behold, here I am; I will readily go. Even from there, I will not cease to proclaim your name with joyous yearning: HURRY AND COME SOON; COME MY LORD JESUS; COME TO JUDGE THE LIVING AND THE DEAD.[27] Amen.

III.
Therefore believe assuredly that these bodies of ours will rise from the dead and will live eternally together with their souls.

Indeed, this I avowed in the articles of my faith, saying, I BELIEVE IN THE RESURRECTION OF THE FLESH AND IN ETERNAL LIFE. For when our LORD Jesus will return on the day of judgment, all people will be gathered before him, the dead and the living, the evil and the pious; then the earth and

---

[24] 1ˢᵗ Timothy 4.

[25] 1ˢᵗ Corinthians 15.

[26] Romans 8.

[27] Revelation 4:8.

the oceans will surrender their dead;[28] and for a moment the souls will return into their deceased bodies, and they will appear alive before the LORD. And we, who are still alive and are left, will be caught up together with them in the clouds to meet the LORD in the air:[29] then the LORD will separate them, like a shepherd, the sheep from the goats; and he will put the goats to his left, the sheep to his right; then he will issue the verdict saying to those at his right, COME, YOU WHO ARE BLESSED BY MY FATHER; TAKE YOUR INHERITANCE, THE KINGDOM PREPARED FOR YOU SINCE THE CREATION OF THE WORLD.[30] But to those at his left he will say, DEPART FROM ME, YOU WHO ARE CURSED, INTO THE ETERNAL FIRE PREPARED FOR THE DEVIL AND HIS ANGELS.[31] And they will enter eternal pain; the righteous, however, will enter eternal life.

If you, dear soul, would like to have more witnesses from scripture, keep the following words in mind:

> Your dead will live, their bodies will rise; wake up and praise, you who dwell under the earth.[32]
>
> Have you not read of the resurrection of the dead, that was told to you by God, saying: I am the God of Abraham, and the God of Isaac, and the God of Jacob. GOD is not a God of the dead but of the living.[33]
>
> Multitudes who sleep under the earth will awake: some to eternal life, others to eternal shame and disgrace.[34]
>
> I know that my Redeemer lives, … and after my skin has been destroyed, yet in my flesh I will see GOD; I myself will see him with my own eyes – I, and not another.[35]

---

[28] Revelation 20:12-13.

[29] 1st Thessalonians 4.

[30] Matthew 25:34.

[31] Matthew 25:41.

[32] Isaiah 26:19.

[33] Exodus 3; Matthew 22:31-32.

[34] Daniel 12:2.

[35] Job 19:25-27.

> Truly, truly, I say to you, a time is coming and has now come when the dead will hear the voice of the Son of God, and those who hear it, they will live.[36]
>
> And this is the will of the one who sent me, that whoever looks to the Son and believes in him shall have eternal life, and I will raise him up at the day of judgment.[37]
>
> I am the resurrection and the life. The one who believes in me will live, even though he dies. And whoever lives by believing in me will never die.[38]

Look also at the following examples, dear soul, and keep in mind how easy it will be for the almighty Lord to raise the dead; for it has always required only a word by him. Behold, when he raised the deceased young man, the widow's only son of Nain, he said, YOUNG MAN, I SAY TO YOU, GET UP![39] Then the dead man sat up, and he was alive. Likewise he also awakened the lifeless little daughter of one of the synagogue leaders, saying, LITTLE GIRL, I SAY TO YOU, GET UP![40] The same also happened with dear Lazarus of Bethany who had been lying in the grave for four days already: LAZARUS, COME FORTH![41] said the LORD. And at once he walked out alive from his grave.

Indeed, my soul, through human understanding and ability, this seems impossible; but with our Lord and God nothing is impossible.[42] Just as a mother knows well into which chamber and bed she has laid her child to rest, and as she returns in the morning to awaken and pick up the child, so does the Lord also know where our bodies –which had been his temple and dwelling– are put to rest; therefore, it will be easier for him to resurrect our dead, cold, and decayed bodies and bones than for a mother to awaken her sleeping child in the cradle.

---

[36] John 5:25.

[37] John 6:39-40.

[38] John 11:25.

[39] Luke 7:14.

[40] Mark 5:41.

[41] John 11:43.

[42] Luke 1:37.

Above all, we have our Lord Jesus Christ –the head of his congregation–[43] not only be our example, but also our predecessor; indeed, he is the origin and the foundation for our resurrection. For he has died for the sake of our sins, and he has been put into the grave; and on the third day he has risen again, joyfully, for our righteousness' sake; and he calls out to us all, saying, FOR BECAUSE I LIVE, YOU WILL ALSO LIVE.[44]

Indeed, my LORD Jesus, because you live, we shall certainly also live, for you are the head, and we are the limbs; and because you have arisen, we will certainly also rise; and since you live as the head, shall we not live as your limbs? That is why I believe, my LORD Jesus, in your joyous arrival, and daily I yearn:

> The last day is almost here,
> On which, like Peter, the LORD will teach to us,
> And heaven and earth will go up in flames.
> Then the world will be terrified,
> When it will see the powerful, brave God
> Arrive so swiftly and so soon.
> How miraculously will one then see
> The dead come out of the graves,
> And everyone will stand in front of the judge.
> No one will be able to hide,
> Every single person must come near
> To hear the judgment.
> Then it will be revealed,
> All that was hidden here;
> That day will make it clear.
> The judge knows the depths of the heart,
> He also bears in mind the person's mouth;
> He will judge righteously at that hour.

---

[43] 1st Corinthians 15.
[44] John 14:19.

This weighs on my mind day and night;
  Because I am a great sinner,
  What shall I do, where shall I go?
Oh Jesus, my faithful savior,
  You will be the judge yourself;
  There – show your faith to me.
Consider your great benevolence
  Which will untie me from my sins,
  Oh Lord, do not drive me away from you.
Your death, your fright, and your severe pain
  Which you alone endured for me,
  Let it not be lost on me.
I plead and shout, oh God my Lord,
  Help that I turn toward you
  Before swift death will come along.
Although my sins had no aim,
  Your mercy is bountiful indeed,
  Which I do not want to chase away.
When Mary had lamented her sins,
  And when the convict shouted undauntedly,
  To neither of them have you refused your mercy.
Help me stand at your right
  Among your dear sheep,
  Let me not remain among the sinners.
When the condemned will depart
  From you into the agonies of hell,
  Then, LORD, lead me into life.
Lord Jesus Christ, my comfort and my joy,
  I await you at all times,
  Do come whenever you want, I am ready,

A M E N.

IV.
For all of humanity, eternal life will indeed be a gloriously joyous life.

 Truly, dear soul, you speak rightly for all the multitudes of human beings; indeed, even for all that which humans believe, think, and imagine. For scripture says, WHAT NO EYE HAS SEEN, NOR EAR HEARD, NOR THE HUMAN HEART CONCEIVED, WHAT GOD HAS PREPARED FOR THOSE WHO LOVE HIM.[45]

Eternal God, what joy, what delight, what glory, what benign existence will be there?[46] Indeed, my soul, who would not keep this in mind every day? Who would not eagerly like to listen, sing, and speak of this? Who would not rather be there and experience such joy? However, who may tell us about it? And where shall we hear about it so that our hearts may be joyous and yearn for it?

Dear soul, even though the great prophet Isaiah as well as the great apostle Paul appear silent, without imparting more about that joy,[47] in many beautiful verses of scripture the Holy Spirit conveys much about the eternal delights which are to be kept in mind, namely:

> Dear friends, now we are children of God, and what we will be
> has not yet been made known; but we know that when Christ
> appears, we shall be like him, for we shall see him as he is.[48]
> In my flesh I shall see God.[49]
> Then the righteous will shine like the sun in the kingdom of their
> Father.[50]

---

[45] 1 Corinthians 2:9; Isaiah 64:4.

[46] Psalm 16.

[47] Isaiah 64; 1 Corinthians 2.

[48] 1 John 3:2.

[49] Job 19:26.

The teachers will shine like the brightness of the heavens, and those who lead many to righteousness, like the stars forever and ever.[51]

GOD will be everything within everything.[52]

And so we will be with the Lord forever.[53]

The Lord will transform our lowly body so that it will be like his glorious body.[54]

At the resurrection people will neither marry nor be given in marriage; they will be like the angels in heaven.[55]

Then I, John, saw the Holy City, the new Jerusalem, coming down out of heaven from God, prepared as a bride who isbeautifully dressed for her husband; and I heard a loud voice from the throne saying, "Look! God's dwelling place is now among the people, and he will dwell with them. They will be his people, and God himself will be with them and be their God. And God will wipe every tear from their eyes, and there will be no more death or suffering or crying or pain, for the old order of things has passed away. And he, who was seated on the throne, said, I am making everything new![56]

And I did not see a temple in the city, because the Lord, the almighty God, is its temple; and the land and the city do not need the sun or the moon to shine on it; for the glory of God gives it light and its lamp is the Lamb; and the nations will walk by its light, and the kings of the earth will bring their splendor into it; and its gates will not be shut during the day, for there will not be night there.[57]

The throne of God and of the Lamb will be in the city, and his servants will serve him; and they will see his face, and his name

---

[50] Matthew 13:43.

[51] Daniel 12:3.

[52] 2 Corinthians 15:28.

[53] 1 Thessalonians 4:17.

[54] Philippians 3:21.

[55] Matthew 22:30.

[56] Revelation 21:2-5.

[57] Revelation 21:22-27.

will be on their foreheads.; and there will be no more night, and they will not need the light of a lamp or the light of the sun, for God, the LORD, will give them light, and they will reign for ever and ever.[58]

All these, dear soul, are only short verses, but they nevertheless are filled with inexpressible kindness. Although scripture provides lengthy sermons thereof, our afflicted hearts may be too weak and our minds too small to grasp it. That is why the Holy Spirit opens only a small window with these short verses to let us glimpse inside, so that we know what we believe and hope, and what we may joyfully anticipate. And whenever we will arrive there, and take in such joy, we will indeed say to each other what Elisabeth said to the Holy Virgin Mary, BLESSED ARE YOU WHO HAS BELIEVED.[59]

Oh eternal life, oh glorious life, oh unending joy and delight, oh eternal Jerusalem, you Holy City of God, you most endearing bride of my LORD Jesus Christ, I love you in my heart, and my being longs for your beauty; oh how beautiful, how glorious, how noble you are! You are most beautiful and no stain is on you. When I think of you, oh Jerusalem –which is above– my heart longs after you, indeed, after my mother Jerusalem, after my fatherland Jerusalem,[60] and after you, LORD Jesus, who is its head, the light, the LORD, the eternal shepherd.

Oh holy life, oh blessed life, which God has prepared for those who love him; oh you vibrant life, you quiet life, you peaceful life, wherein there will be neither death, nor grief, nor sin, nor pain, nor fright, nor ailment, nor fear, nor change. A life full of beauty and glory, without adversary, without sinful desires; where there is perfect love and no fright; where there is an eternal day and one spirit beholding God from face to face; and where every heart is abundantly nourished with the food of life. I desire to see your luminescence, and my heart yearns

---

[58] Revelation 22:3-5.
[59] Luke 1:45.
[60] Galatians 4:25-27.

after your blissfulness. The more I have you in my mind, the more I ache from the love that I bear for you.

Oh, good for you, my soul, when you will dissolve from your earthly body, and when you journey freely toward heaven; how soundly will you arrive! how endearingly will you be received! you will be calm and safe eternally, and you will neither fear enemies nor death. Indeed, at all times you will be with the Lord, your God and Savior; you will have him present always,[61] and you will look at him unceasingly,[62] who is the most beautiful among all humans. Do you not hear, my soul, how he calls for you, and how he speaks with a blissful voice, ARISE, MY DARLING, MY BEAUTIFUL ONE, COME WITH ME. SEE, THE WINTER IS PAST; THE RAINS ARE OVER AND GONE. ARISE, MY DARLING, AND COME HERE, MY BEAUTIFUL ONE, COME WITH ME, MY CHOSEN ONE; I DESIRE YOUR BEAUTY; COME AND BE JOYFUL IN MY PRESENCE WITH MY AN-GELS, WHOSE COMPANY I HAVE PROMISED YOU; COME HERE FROM YOUR MANY TRAVAILS AND DANGERS; AND ENTER INTO YOUR LORD'S JOYOUSNESS.[63]

Oh, rejoice, my soul, and be cheerful, you beautiful prince's daughter,[64] for the King requests your beauty, and the most beautiful among humans loves your adornment.[65] All best to you, my soul, all best to you for ever and ever; when I behold you, oh, magnificent life, your glory, your salvation, your beauty,[66] your gates and walls, your streets and many dwellings, your citizens and your mighty king, my most ingratiating LORD Jesus Christ in his adornment; for your walls are made of precious stones, your gates of exquisite pearls, your streets of pure gold in which the beautiful *hallelujah* is sung without ceasing. There will be nothing of which we suffer and that we see in this miserable life. Within you, there is no darkness, no night, and there are no distinctive epochs. Within you, no one walks with lanterns, neither

---

[61] 1ˢᵗ Thessalonians 4.

[62] Psalm 45.

[63] Song of Solomon 2.

[64] Song of Solomon 7.

[65] Psalm 45.

[66] Revelation 12.

moon nor stars will shine; but God from God, light from light, and the sun of righteousness will shine for you eternally.[67] The white and immaculate Lamb of God is your brightest and most beautiful light. The countenance of your most beautiful King, which you will always behold, is your sun, your luminescence, and all your delight; indeed, the King of kings himself is with you, and his servants are around him.

There are the choirs of angels, which praise God. There is the congregation of heavenly citizens. There is an eternal, delightful feast for all who have arrived from this troublesome pilgrimage to your joyousness. There are sheep and lambs which have escaped the snares of this world; they rejoice indeed in their eternal Fatherland; although unequal in adornment and glory, they live with the same joyousness. There the right and perfect love will reign;[68] for God is everything in all which they will behold without ceasing; and with a steadfast heart they will love and praise him, praise and love him; and all their doing is to praise God without end, without ceasing, and without any exertion.

Oh, how well I will be in eternity, when I will hear the heavenly music after this life which the citizens in the heavenly fatherland will play to praise and honor the eternal King. Oh, good, good for me, when I will also play the same, and when I will stand next to my King, next to my God and Lord; and when I will behold him in his glory, as he has promised me himself, saying, FATHER, I WANT THOSE YOU HAVE GIVEN ME TO BE WITH ME WHERE I AM, AND TO SEE MY GLORY, THE GLORY YOU HAVE GIVEN ME BECAUSE YOU LOVED ME BEFORE THE CREATION OF THE WORLD.[69]

AS THE DEER PANTS FOR THE STREAMS OF WATER, SO MY SOUL PANTS FOR YOU, LORD, MY GOD. MY SOUL THIRSTS FOR YOU, MY LORD, FOR THE LIVING GOD. WHEN WILL I GET THERE SO THAT I CAN BEHOLD YOUR COUNTENANCE?[70] Oh, you fountain of life, you well of all com-

---

[67] Malachi 4:2.
[68] 1st Corinthians 15.
[69] John 17:24.
[70] Psalm 42:1-2.

fort and all joy, when may I drink from the living water of your comfort? When shall I leave this miserable valley of tears and see your glory? My Lord and my God, how my soul is yearning, is thirsting for you! When shall I arrive and appear in your presence?

LORD Jesus, my comfort, my joy, my delight; you most endearing, most beautiful, most blissful in my eyes, let me see the day of eternal delight, the day of joy and of salvation which you have made, on which we shall rejoice and be cheerful.[71] Oh, what a clear, beautiful, bright, and pleasant day this will be – lasting forever with no evening approaching. On this day I will hear joy and delight, rejoicing and gratefulness forever and ever.

Enter, my soul, into your Lord's joy;[72] enter, my love, into his eternal delight, into the house of the LORD your God, which is full of great joys that are glorious and inexpressible and that have no end; enter into his joy where there will be no more sadness, but eternal delight; where you will have everything your heart desires and where no heartbreak will take place.

This will be eternal life – the kind, cheerful life that will last forever. There, no enemy will pursue us, and no evil desires will tempt us. Instead, there will be great peace and assured calmness; gentle, quiet, and kind delight; cheerful being and exquisite glory, eternal salvation and the Holy Trinity, one eternal deity in three persons and three persons in one eternal deity; which we shall behold in eternity; and we shall rejoice in the Lord, our God, forever.

Oh joy above all joys; oh delight above all delights, to which nothing is comparable. When shall I enter to behold my God who lives in you? I want to go there and see such great glory.

Come, dear Lord Jesus, come, and do not delay; come Lord, my Savior; come Lord, you comfort of all nations; come my light and my Redeemer, lead my soul from the dungeon of this misery, so that I get there and praise your holy name.

---

[71] Psalm 18.
[72] Matthew 25.

Oh eternal kingdom, oh imperishable heavenly kingdom, within you is eternal light, and the peace of God which is higher than all understanding and reason;[73] within you rest the souls of the righteous; eternal joy is above their heads;[74] they are surrounded with blissfulness and jubilation; however, fright and misery is far from them. Lord, my God, how glorious is your heavenly kingdom in which all the righteous reign together with you; they are clothed with light and bright splendor; they wear golden crowns on their heads;[75] they behold you face to face, and you please them over and over with your peace.

This is eternal delight and not grief; this is eternal joy and not suffering; this is eternal wellbeing and not tribulation; this is an eternally kind existence and not arduousness; this is the eternal light and not darkness; this is eternal life and not death; this is pure youthfulness and not agedness; this is pure ornamentation and not ailment; this is pure decoration and not unsightliness; this is pure health and not illness; this is pure jubilation without ceasing; there, no one knows of pain; there, no sighing is heard; there, no sorrow is known; they soar in eternal joy, and they may not fear any evil.

For there is the eternal God – nothing less than recognizing God the LORD and seeing him face to face. Blessed eternally are those who have been saved from this arduous, dangerous life, and who have arrived at your eternal, great joyousness:

> Cheerfully I sing
>   When I contemplate such joy,
> I walk in great leaps,
>   My heart laughs with joy,
> My being rises up high,
>   Powerfully from this world,
> I yearn for those things,
>   but what's of this world, I disregard,
>   A M E N

---

[73] Philippians 4.
[74] Isaiah 35.
[75] 2nd Timothy 4.

V.

Where, however, will the ungodly people end up, and how will they fare?

They will enter eternal agony with body and soul.[76] Indeed, dear soul, just as eternal joy and delight – wherein the chosen will soar– remains inexpressible, so can no one surmise the inexpressible fright and torture in which the ungodly and the condemned are eternally tormented and punished. The prophets –when speaking of hell's eternal agony of the condemned– summarize the punishment in three distinct words: *Ibi erit,* they say, *poenarum multiplicitas, acerbitas, aternitas.*[77]

I.

Firstly, the agony and fright of the condemned in hell will be manifold, and there will be so many punishments that no one can count them. For scripture says, THEY WILL BE THROWN INTO THE DARKNESS, WHERE THERE WILL BE WEEPING AND GNASHING OF TEETH.[78] THEY WILL BE IN HELL AND IN TORMENT.[79] ON THE WICKED, THE LORD WILL RAIN LIGHTNING AND BURNING SULFUR; AND REWARD THEM WITH A HORRIBLE TEMPEST.[80] FOR THE WORMS THAT EAT THEM WILL NOT DIE, THE FIRE THAT BURNS THEM WILL NOT BE QUENCHED, AND THEY SHALL BE LOATHSOME TO ALL MANKIND.[81] TERROR WILL SEIZE THEM, PAIN AND ANGUISH WILL GRIP THEM; THEY WILL WRITHE LIKE A WOMAN IN LABOR. THEY WILL LOOK AGHAST AT

---

[76] Matthew 25.

[77] There will be *manifold, harsh,* and *eternal* punishments.

[78] Matthew, 25:30.

[79] Luke 16:23.

[80] Psalm 11:6.

[81] Isaiah 66:24.

EACH OTHER, THEIR FACES AFLAME.[82] MAGGOTS ARE SPREAD OUT
BENEATH THEM AND WORMS COVER THEM.[83]

Behold, dear soul, with these and similar verses, scripture
points out to the ungodly that all suffering, all misery, all sorrow, all tribulation, all torment, all agony, hunger, grief, fright,
affliction, thirst, heat, frost, sickness, pain, death, perdition,
wasting away, dejection, and whatever else that can neither be
named nor voiced – all this will become their eternal company,
and all the horrid devils will be their henchmen.

II.

Secondly, they say, *Ibi erit poenarum acerbitas*. That
means: the manifold frights and hellish agonies will be
so harsh and terrifying, so bitter and rough, that not
one of the doomed can bear it, even though they must bear it in
all eternity; for scripture says, OF FRIGHT THEY WILL SEEK DEATH
BUT WILL NOT FIND IT; THEY WILL LONG TO DIE, BUT DEATH WILL
ELUDE THEM.[84] Indeed, dear soul, there will be neither life nor
death; between life and death they will be tormented and
plagued in inexpressible woe and anguish. Like a glowing mol-
ten mass in a smelting furnace, so will the doomed be scorched,
frightened, shattered, smashed, and stricken eternally.

III.

Thirdly, the generations of old say, *Ibi erit poenarum
aternitas*. That means: their manifold and unbearable
fright and anguish will not last for a limited time only,
nor will it last long, for long is not eternal. Instead, says the
LORD, THEY WILL GO AWAY TO ETERNAL PUNISHMENT.[85] Indeed,
my soul, if it would merely last long, then it would come to an

---

[82] Isaiah 13:8.

[83] Isaiah 14:11.

[84] Revelation 9:6.

[85] Matthew 25:46.

end eventually. Eternity, however, has no end. FOR THEIR LAND WILL TURN TO BLAZING TAR, WHICH WILL NOT BE QUENCHED, NEITHER BY DAY NOR BY NIGHT; ITS SMOKE WILL RISE FOREVER.[86] AND THE SMOKE OF THEIR TORMENT WILL RISE FOREVER AND EVER, AND THERE WILL BE NO REST, NEITHER DAY NOR NIGHT.[87]

Consider, dear soul, lying forever on a soft bed, being sustained by fine, magnificent nourishment and refreshment within a wonderfully glorious hall; and yet, being tied down to that bed and not being able to leave it forever. Truly, one would not even wish to be alive! There, however, the doomed shall not wallow in wantonness, but in eternal woe and anguish, in frightening fetidness and darkness; and they will not find a crumb or a drop of refreshment in all of eternity.

Oh, do listen, you poor, miserable child of the world; listen and take this to heart; you – who loves the world and its desires, saying, *how delightful to be in this world, how delightful to be in this world!* – understand that the time will come –and it certainly is not far away– when you will say together with the rich, doomed man, *oh, I suffer great anguish in these flames.* Instead, you will lament and say, *oh, it is awful to be here, it is awful to be here*; yet, you will have to stay there for all eternity. You will suffer eternally, and you will never be able to get out; there you will waste away forever and, yet, you will never die; you will suffer unutterable agony of which there will be no end.

Oh, LORD Jesus Christ, grant all ears to hear and all hearts to understand; grant that I diligently listen to your faithful messengers, that I do penance, and that I put aside the deeds of darkness;[88] grant me not to assume the image of this world so that I will not be plunged into hell's eternal agony. Govern, teach, and guide me through your Holy Spirit, so that I learn daily to live as a Christian; and, whenever it pleases you, that I die blessedly; so that I will not be delivered to the place of eternal pain and anguish; but that I may inherit and own

---

[86] Isaiah 34:9.

[87] Revelation 14:11.

[88] Romans 13:12.

eternal, joyful life together with you, LORD, my savior, and with all your saints.

LORD God, through your benevolence,
   Lead me on the rightful path;
LORD Christ, protect me well,
   So that I will not go astray;
Hold me firmly in my faith,
   At this dreadful time;
Grant me to steadfastly prepare myself,
   For the wedding and its eternal joy,

A M E N,   A M E N.

APPENDIX

PREFACE

by
Martin Moller

To the noble, very honorable, virtuous, and devoted Lady, POLYXENA, born Nächerin of Buchwald, widow of the noble, virtuous Lord Balthasar Bucklers of Groditz of honorable memory, patrimonial heir of Falckenberg, Kutaw and Cantersdorff, etc., and their bequeathed descendants of my most beneficent Lady.

Grace and peace, through Jesus Christ our LORD.

Dle / viel Ehren thugendreiche / Gestrenge Fraw / Es ist offenbar / das alles / Noble, very honorable, virtuous, and devoted Lady. It is apparent that everything a Christian person shall study, retain, and do from God's word is comprised in learning how

1st to live in a Christian manner,

and

2nd to die blessedly.

The royal prophet David has both articles in mind when he says, LORD, TEACH US TO KEEP IN MIND THAT WE MUST DIE, SO THAT WE WILL BECOME WISE.[1] ly, the wise man Sirach admonishes, WHATEVER YOU DO, KEEP THE END IN MIND; THEN YOU WILL NEVERMORE DO WICKED THINGS.[2]

For what is a Christian life? Nothing else than when a human contemplates his uncertain end, practices daily the right-

---

[1] Psalm 90:12.
[2] Sirach 7:36.

eous cognizance of God, lives in true penance, practices his faith, keeps his conscience pure, so that he (says Sirach) will never again do wicked things. That is, he will not, at any moment, let himself be found in a state unworthy of attaining salvation. And what does it mean – to die blessedly? A Christian shall daily keep in mind not only his mortality and his unprotected exposure to death anywhere, but also his departure in a manner of remaining a sure heir of eternal salvation at every hour and every moment.

That is the righteous wisdom of which David speaks; indeed, it is the best wisdom and art, which has been revealed to Christians alone, and which may be learned nowhere except from God's word. However, since learning such a blessed art of dying does not stand within our powers, but is a gift of God, the man of God prescribes to us the ardent yearning of daily prayer to God,[3] teaching us to keep in mind that we must die so that we become wise. That is, may he give us the grace through his Holy Spirit to learn from his Holy Word to conduct and to conclude our lives here temporally in such a way that we may live there eternally.

The heathen of the past did not know this holy art of dying; and it is concealed still today to all who do not accept Jesus Christ, our LORD, as their Savior. For even though Cicero spoke of experience, *vita tam turpis ne morti quidem honestae locum relinquit;*[4] which means: just as an honorable life is generally followed by an honorable death, so a wicked, shameful life will generally bring a wicked, shameful death; there is, however, a momentous difference, *inter vitam honestam, et inter Christianam; inter mortem honestam; et inter Christianam sive salutarem;* that is, between an honorable, upright, outward conduct of life and a Christian conduct of life; and between an honorable death and a blessed departure.

---

[3] Psalm 90.

[4] Cicero, *Orat. pro P. Quinctio*, 49. "*... but a life so foul leaves its place not even for an honorable death ...*"

When Emperor Augustus had implored Euthanasian daily – hoping to find a pleasant death–, he understood it to be nothing more than leaving behind an honest name on account of both, his conduct of life and his death. When, however, he and other heathen faced death, there was no comfort, no hope; instead, there was much fright and fear; and they found their end, as Virgil said, *Vitaque cum gemitu fugit indignata sub umbras;*[5] that is, unwillingly he let go of life, and he journeyed without comfort into the agony of hell.

That is why the writings of the unbelievers contain only pointless lamentations about human misery, about the short time of our lives, and about death. They remain silent about any comfort, *Totum, quod est homo miseria est,* says one of them; that is, there is nothing more to being human except much tribulation and misery. King Xerxes cried bitter tears when he looked at the beautiful throng of his young, fresh army; and he pondered that not one of them in this beautiful, large assembly would reach the age of one hundred years. Aristotle lamented death, saying: *Omnium terribilium terribilissimum est mors;*[6] that is, among everything terrible and horrendous on earth, there is nothing more frightful than death. The heathen' books are full of such and similar dreary whimpering and wailing.

We also find that several among them have sought and searched for counsel against the fear of death, whether there might be something to soothe one's heart in such fright and to surrender oneself willingly to dying. However, they did not get beyond what Seneca said: *Effice mortem tibi cogitatione familiarem, et, si ita sors tulerit, posses illi obviamire;*[7] that is, you must thoroughly imagine death and always keep it in mind, so that you can willingly surrender whenever it takes place. That is why we read that the Egyptians had a custom –during their

---

[5] Virgil, *Ultimo Aeneid,* XII, 953. *"And (his) life with a resentful groan fled below (into) the shadows."*

[6] Herodotus, *Polymnia.*

[7] Seneca, *Naturales Quaestiones.*

banquets and feasts– of presenting an image of a dead person in a coffin to the guests and adding the words, *In hunc intuens, bibe et sis animo hilari, post mortem enim tale eris;*[8] that is, oh, look at this image and drink and make merry; keep in mind, however, that death will also turn you into a likeness of this image. And that was their *preparatio* – their preparation for dying willingly.

Such art was employed by Agag, the ungodly Amalekite King. When he saw that the prophet Samuel wanted to put him to death, he confidently went to him, saying, THUS, THE BITTERNESS OF DEATH IS DISPELLED.[9] As if he were trying to say, one day such a fall must take place; let it be rather sooner, since this will be a wicked hour indeed. Meanwhile, the heathen' hearts trembled; they found no comfort, and they went down raging and griping against God. For even though they had searched at length for comfort to soothe their hearts, they ended up just as Cicero said, *Ego tentatis rebus omnibus, nihil inuenio, in quo acquiescam;*[10] that is, I have brought forth all the arts which I had ever studied, so that I would be able to attain some comfort, but I do not find any.

However, when they saw the apprehension of the dying, or their despair regarding death, they continued to mock them, saying, *O te dementem, et oblitum fragilitatis tuae, si tunc times mortem, cum tonat;*[11] that is, you fool, have you not previously considered that you must die; will you only fear death now that it comes roaring along?

With respect to eternal life, Plato, Cicero, and others made great efforts in claiming that the souls of humans are immortal (as for their bodies, no one has even considered that they may rise again and live), and that the souls of the pious would have a place of rest. Indeed, Cicero even attempted to encourage

---

[8] Herodotus, *Euterpe*, chapter 78.

[9] 1st Samuel 15:32c.

[10] Cicero, *Epistulae*.

[11] Seneca, *Naturales Quaestiones*.

them, imagining that he will rejoice when arriving at the assembly of souls, saying: *O praeclarum diem, cum ad illud duvunum concilium coetumque proficiscar, et cum ex hac turba et coluvione discedam;*[12] that is, oh, what a glorious day this will be, when I will depart from this arduous life and attend the assembly of souls. However, since the heathen have no true faith, no bearing on the Holy Spirit, and no hope or permanent comfort, the courage they attain in such manner will yield no assurance, but only impermanence and doubtfulness. And likewise, Cicero, saying, *Quod si hoc erro, quod hominum animos immortales esse credo, libenter erro, non mihi hunc errorem, quo delector, dum viuo extorqueri volo;*[13] that is, if I should err in deeming the souls of humans to be immortal, then I will gladly do so; since such an error pleases me well, I will not let it be taken from me as long as I live.

 The heathen did not get any further, and they found no additional comfort or preparation for death, and –to this day– neither do all the hypocrites and all the impenitent who have no true faith in Jesus Christ our Lord.

Indeed, even the hypocrites, the unbelievers, and the impenitent among the Christians shall keep well in mind that their damnation on that day will be much more severe and much greater than that of the heathen, since the light of the Gospels shines more brightly on them than on the heathen; nevertheless, they will not do penance, remaining *noluerunt;* that is, unwilling. For thus speaks the Lord himself, IF ANYONE WILL NOT WELCOME YOU OR LISTEN TO YOUR WORDS, LEAVE THAT HOME OR TOWN AND SHAKE THE DUST OFF YOUR FEET. TRULY I TELL YOU: IT WILL BE MORE BEARABLE FOR SODOM AND GOMORRAH ON THE DAY OF JUDGMENT THAN FOR THAT TOWN.[14] ANYONE WHO HAS EARS, LET HIM LISTEN.[15]

---

[12] Cicero, *de Senectute.*
[13] Ibid.
[14] Matthew 10:14-15.
[15] Matthew 13:9.

Here one shall contemplate in all urgency and diligence the most significant difference between a believing, penitent human life and death and an unbelieving, impenitent human life and death, so that we know the grace of God which has been given to us Christians, and that we learn to acclaim and praise him wholeheartedly.

I.

1st. Regarding firstly the life of humans, the unbelieving hypocrite has no righteous cognizance of God; he looks at heaven like cows staring at the new barn door; he regards the noble creations of God like hogs regarding acorns under the tree; he does not even consider that he owes gratitude to God for his life and his wellbeing; he does not inquire about eternal life, but he follows his heart's desire only to live forever here where he can indulge in the desires of his flesh. And he is certain that such livestock, even hogs, lead a better life than those humans who have been created in the image of God. The faithful, penitent Christian person, on the other hand, knows the Lord, his creator, and he rejoices in having found faith in God; he makes use of all gifts of God with gratitude; he praises God, who has created everything so well and wisely; he keeps in mind day and night that he too may come to his God and live with him forever.[16]

2nd. The unbelieving person –whenever he hears about God punishing a wicked life with a terrible death– thinks: in preparing for death, it would be quite sufficient to apply oneself to outward honor and not to live in openly egregious sin. Or he keeps saying together with the Pharisee, I THANK YOU GOD THAT I AM NOT LIKE OTHER PEOPLE, ROBBERS, THE UNJUST, ADULTERERS, etc.,[17] presuming readily that if there were an eternal life, God would not deny it to him for being an honorable person. The faithful Christian, on the other hand, will study the salutary

---

[16] Acts 17.
[17] Luke 18:11.

art of dying;[18] he will recognize and wholeheartedly repent his sins;[19] he will find comfort in his Savior's accomplishment and merit, and he will have joyous confidence and delightful hope that GOD will accept his penance of sins;[20] and he will live like this daily, maintaining his faith and a good conscience until the end.[21]

3rd. The hypocritical children of the world –because they are doing well– will pretend to be good Christians and speak much about trust in God and also about other teachings, such as being patient in suffering; they will become secure and defiant, and they will presume that they would never have to lay down. When, however, the hour of tribulation will arrive, and when one deluge after the other will come in thunderously, all their courage will soon fade away; the skies will break and the earth will go under.[22] They know of no comfort, and they will not listen to others who try to aid them with comfort; instead, they will impatiently sing Gideon's song, Why –if the LORD is with us– are we doing so dreadfully?[23] The heart of the faithful Christian, on the other hand, has made the calculation a long time ago that it will enter the Kingdom of God not through good days and idle welfare, but through much suffering and tribulation. That is why – whenever a Christian is doing well– he thanks God for allowing him to enjoy the good of the land;[24] he safeguards himself from security;[25] HE SERVES GOD THE LORD IN FEAR AND CELEBRATES HIS RULE WITH TREMBLING.[26] Whenever he is fearful, then he sings together with dear Job, IF WE ACCEPT GOOD FROM THE HAND OF THE LORD, WHY SHALL WE NOT ALSO ACCEPT THE EVIL?[27] If the suffering persists, then he

---

[18] Psalm 90.

[19] Sirach 7.

[20] Wisdom 12.

[21] 1st Timothy.

[22] Psalm 42.

[23] Judges 6.

[24] Acts 14.

[25] Isaiah 1.

[26] Psalm 2:11.

[27] Job 2:10.

sings together with dear David: my soul waits – whether the suffering lasts into the night, whether it lasts into the morning –, my heart shall neither doubt nor worry about God's redeeming power.[28] And if it becomes more and more difficult, he speaks together with Saint Paul, GOD IS FAITHFUL; AND WILL NOT LET YOU BE TRIED BEYOND THAT WHICH YOU CAN BEAR.[29] If flesh and blood become frightened, and if suffering becomes unbearable, he believes and knows THAT FOR THOSE WHO LOVE GOD, ALL THINGS WORK TOGETHER FOR THE GOOD.[30]

4th. The unbeliever and the child of the world –when he is mindful how much death takes from him, having to leave behind everything: God, honor and glory, wife, child, hearth, home, and when he has to run off naked– will begin to lament: oh death, oh death, how bitter you are, etc.[31] He will despair and say together with the Emperor Severus: *Omnia fui, et nihil mihi prodest;*[32] that is, I was great, glorious, mighty and more; but now when I must die, I have nothing at all which could rescue me. The righteous Christian person, on the other hand, has chosen the right and beneficial part; he rejoices in the exuberant wealth of the eternal goods of God; he can let go of the temporal at any moment and say together with King David, LORD, YOU HAVE PUT GLADNESS IN MY HEART MORE THAN THEIR GRAIN AND WINE CORN ABOUND.[33]

5th. The impenitent hypocrite –when he becomes sick– only thinks about where he may have caught the illness, what unhealthy food he may have eaten, where he may have had a bad drink, where he may have been either too cold, or too hot, or too exposed. He is angry and impatient about having ended up in such misfortune. The believer, however, knows that not a hair

---

[28] Psalm 130.

[29] 1st Corinthians 10:13b.

[30] Romans 8:28.

[31] Sirach 41.

[32] Ae. Spartianus. *"I was everything, but nothing is of use to me."*

[33] Psalm 4:7.

can fall from his head without the will of his God,[34] much less that he should lose the noble gift of health without the particular will of God. For that reason he faults his sins with which he has earned the punishment of illness,[35] and he recognizes that God chastises and thereby urges him to do penance; and he knows well that when God intends to afflict a person, all causes of illness rest with the fault of sin.

6th. The unbelieving, self-assured person of the world does not keep his soul in mind until he becomes ill; only then does he intend to become pious. Previously, throughout his life, he stayed away from preachers; now, however, he swiftly calls for the preacher. Previously he called him a parson – indeed, a wavering, useless parson; now, however, he calls him a dignified servant of God, and he cries out to him: oh, dear, pious, honorable sir, help me, give me good counsel so that I will not be damned. This person would rather start with the *Deus in audiutorium* instead of the *Benedicamus,* as it is stated in several of our hymns: after always mocking the grace of God, I fear that it will scarcely hover above him. The faithful, penitent Christian, however, is ready at all hours and at every moment;[36] he sits in daily preparedness for dying blessedly; he will not let himself be found at any hour or moment in such a state or condition of heart, in which he would not dare to be saved; and wherever he goes, wherever he stands, he can say with a joyously cheerful heart: LORD Jesus Christ, my comfort and friend, I wait for you always; come whenever you will, I am ready. And when suffering even a trivial assault, he joyfully readies himself: LORD, LET YOUR SERVANT NOW JOURNEY IN PEACE.[37]

7th. The unbeliever and hypocrite –whenever needing counsel and help in illness– is not concerned whether it is provided by the devil or some conjurer, saying, *Flectere si nequeo superos,*

---

[34] Matthew 10.
[35] Jeremiah 10.
[36] Psalm 90.
[37] Luke 2:29.

Acheronta mouebo;[38] that is, if God does not help, so let the devil help or whoever is available, as long as I am being helped. The faithful, God-fearing Christian, however, knows that God has strictly forbidden all wayward means and superstition;[39] and he knows well that Satan's cunning through his conjurers and spell-sayers will do no good to anyone, but only usurp their souls and tear them away from God.[40] Indeed, the Christian believes and knows that it is a thousand times better to die in God's name than to be healthy and live in the devil's name.[41] That is why he will apply only the means ordered by God, so that his God will not be tempted. And if he cannot obtain them, or if God withholds the blessing, then he will speak: LORD Jesus, here I am, do with me according to your good pleasure; if it is your will,[42] you will help me indeed; and if it is not pleasing to you, here I am; your will, my God, I will carry out willingly.[43]

8th. In illness, the child of the world will not keep God's word in mind for he has not learned it; he knows to find comfort neither in his Holy Baptism nor in Holy Communion. Some have worldly histories and entertaining stories read to them; some also engage in foolish games to make the heart merry so that they hold back thoughts of death. The believing Christian, however, is experienced in God's word; he knows how to share it rightly[44] and to apply the Laws and Gospels; he delights in the covenant of mercy,[45] which he entered with his GOD at his Holy Baptism; he thirsts after the Lord's Supper, through which he is rightly blessed and restored, and from which he obtains new comfort and joy from Christ; all worldly things become ungainly; he does not seek en-

---

[38] Virgilius 7, *Aeneid.* "*If I am not able to bend those (gods) above, I will move the infernal regions [Acheron, a river in Hades].*"

[39] Exodus 20.

[40] 1st Samuel 13.

[41] Job 12.

[42] Matthew 8.

[43] Psalm 40.

[44] 2nd Timothy.

[45] Acts 8.

tertainment, but he speaks without ceasing of Christ, his Redeemer, and of eternal life; and he looks joyously forward to the blessed hour.

II.

1st. Furthermore, in regard to death and dying: when the heathen or the unbelieving hypocrite recognizes through daily occurring examples that he as well as everyone else must have daily awareness of death, he readies himself by lamenting the harsh misery of humans and the short time of this arduous life – and in doing so, he is not wrong. However, he does not prepare at all for dying; he does not get ready for penance; rather, he gripes and he thinks that God is unjust for letting people die so soon. A righteously believing Christian, on the other hand, reminds himself daily of his mortality, grieves heartily about the original transgression of humans;[46] he weeps about his own sinfulness and wickedness which caused this just punishment of death to come over us; and he says with a humbled heart: *Iram Domini portabo, quia peccavi ei*; that is, I will gladly bear the wrath of the Lord, for I have sinned against him.[47] And again, LORD, YOU ARE RIGHTEOUS, AND YOUR JUDGMENTS ARE RIGHT.[48] In doing so, he honors God, the Lord; he trust that God will not treat us unjustly; and he prepares himself daily for the blessed hour.

2nd. The unbelieving hypocrite –when his human heart contemplates death– is upset, and he is frightened of the sight of death; he trembles and is afraid –since flesh and blood cannot do otherwise– because death is our enemy, and it will strangle us all. The righteously believing person, however, opens the eyes of faith; he beholds death, not according to God's Law, but according to the holy Gospel; he comforts himself and rejoices in his dear LORD Jesus Christ, who has tasted the bitterness of death for him, who has transformed death into a gentle sleep;[49] and he has the joyous assur-

---

[46] Ecclesiastes 3.
[47] Micah 7.
[48] Psalm 119:137.
[49] John 11.

ance that he will not die, but fall asleep gently, and that –through the sweetness of the comfort of Jesus Christ– he will not become aware of the bitterness of death.

3rd. The unbelieving hypocrite –when he contemplates how terribly and abominably death will mangle him and turn him into a malformed, cold corpse being buried in the unfriendly earth– begins to grieve, and all courage vanishes from him; yet, he cannot fare better than King Xerxes, who –as he contemplated death– raised a new subject to put death out of his mind: *Missa hac faciamus, inquit, neque tristium rerum mentionem faciamus, cum iucunda in manibus habeamus;*[50] that is, let this gloomy talk of dying end, and let us take up something else which brings more joy. The righteous believer, on the other hand, sees – *plus ultra*– straight through all the repulsiveness of death, and through the inhospitality of the grave; he disregards how terribly death will mangle his body and to which degree it will decay; instead, he sees how he will come forth gloriously and imperishably; and how he will become like the transfigured body of Jesus Christ, his Savior.

4th. The unbelieving heathen or hypocrite –when he seeks to safeguard himself from death– will not get further than imagining that he would seize renewed courage, that death will only be a small step taken quickly, and that at some time death will simply have to come about.[51] The believer and the righteous person, however, does not trust in the courage of his own flesh, but he trusts in the comfort and courage of the Holy Spirit who lives in him; and he knows for certain that God's peace –which he has tasted through faith and which is higher than all understanding–[52] will keep true his heart and his mind in Christ Jesus until eternal salvation.

5th. The unbelieving hypocrite –when death approaches– stands completely defenseless; there is no faith, no hope, and indeed not one word of assurance which he believes; there is

---

[50] *"Let us do the things sent in this (way), he said, and let us not make mention of sad things, while we might have pleasant things in hand."*

[51] 1st Samuel 15.

[52] Philippians 4.

no comfort to which he can cling to soothe his heart; instead, he feels needless fear and needless fright; and he cannot benefit from God. The faithful Christian, however, has his heart full of faith, full of hope, and full of inexpressible yearning,[53] so that he resides already more in eternal than in temporal life. Moreover, he has the comforting true word of God, which neither lies nor deceives; he envelops it in his heart, he retains it, keeps it safe, and knows that the word will be carried out according to its promise and nothing else; and he says with a joyful heart: LORD Jesus, whoever keeps your word will nevermore see death.[54]

6th. The unbeliever laments –when subjected to the power of death– that he is abandoned, that all the good friends and brothers stay away, and that no one is going to help him. The faithful person, on the other hand, says: Lord, if only I have you, I do not ask for anything under heaven and earth.[55] And even if my body and soul languish, you are indeed GOD, my heart's comfort and my portion. For God knows well that humans cannot persist in affliction; their help, even if it is wonderful, will come to an end. For that reason, when the help of all humans has ended, the faithful person believes and knows that God stands by him; indeed, he has the Holy Trinity in his heart;[56] and around his bed of infirmity, he has many holy angels awaiting his soul.[57]

7th. The unbelievers and the ungodly persons –when they hear that the soul is immortal, and that after this life there will be another life where the righteous will have eternal bliss, the unrighteous, however, eternal damnation and pain–[58] become frightened beyond all measure; they wish this to be untrue and think that no one would ever arise from death; for their unbelieving heart tells them: if that is true, you must be damned

---

[53] Romans 8.
[54] John 8:52.
[55] Psalm 73.
[56] John 14.
[57] Luke 16.
[58] Matthew 25.

eternally. That is why they wish never to have been born. The believing children of God, however, rejoice heartily, and they are delighted that eternal life is prepared for them; they long for it; they wish for it; they yearn for the future with Christ; they only wish that this miserable life would soon end, and that eternal life would begin, since their hope of being redeemed to a much better life is assured.[59]

In suchlike manner, many more contrasts and distinctions can be made to show the great disparity between the conduct of a disbeliever or heathen –even if it appears glorious– and the conduct of a righteous Christian; and furthermore, to show the difference in how the faithful depart from this world as opposed to the impenitent hypocrites and children of the world.[60]

This shall be contemplated most seriously by every person, applied daily with great diligence, and not ceased until he has examined himself thoroughly –and until he knows that he has righteous true faith in Jesus Christ, his Savior– so that he holds him as his greatest treasure, and that he finds all desire and delight in him.[61] Indeed, he shall not lay his head on a pillow until –through diligent prayer and perpetual exercising of faith through the power of the Holy Spirit–[62] he loves the eternal more than the temporal,[63] until he is seriously opposing sin,[64] and until he only desires righteousness; so that he will rightfully recognize the futile misery of this sinful life; that he disregards its splendor and glory;[65] that he yearns for eternal bliss; that he loves Jesus Christ wholeheartedly; that he wishes for his future daily; that he carries out his vocation daily with a

---

[59] Romans 5; Philippians 1.

[60] Luke 16.

[61] 1st Corinthians 3.

[62] 2nd Timothy 4.

[63] 1st John 2.

[64] 1st Timothy 6.

[65] John 21.

good conscience; and that he will be ready at any hour to be released and to come to a revered completion of his work.

For this is the rightful preparation for dying blessedly; and accordingly, we shall always distinguish ourselves from the unbelievers, the impenitent hypocrites, and the children of the world;[66] several of whom know nothing about the LORD Christ; several of whom know a little; several of whom have heard and know about him, but do not know him as their Savior;[67] and several of whom are good Christians only by what they say, but not with their hearts; they boast about their faith, but they do not reveal it; they talk about eternal life, but they do not learn how to attain it.

However, if all this is to be learned, then one must read it, hear it, remember it, and also practice it.[68] Available to us – thankfully– is the endearing and beautiful book of God, the Holy Bible, which everyone –who wishes to do so– can not only have but also read. Other beautiful, endearing books regarding Holy Scripture and the Church Fathers have been put together, in German and in Latin, in which one can find useful teachings, salutary comfort, and helpful admonitions necessary for a Christian life and a blessed dying.

 This, however, I must say: I have held this sacred office of preaching for over twenty-one years now, and while I find these books in part to be good manuals, they nevertheless require more elucidations for unsophisticated readers. While some of them are helpful books of comfort, they often lack instruction about how the guileless heart should find application; and other books are much too lofty, full of contentions and controversies, written more for scholars rather than laypersons.

For that reason, it was my intention many years ago to bring such a book to light in which the common layperson would

---

66 1st Corinthians 6.

67 Matthew 1.

68 Luke 8.

find not only all the most important teaching, comfort, and exhortation, but also good, simple instruction on how to apply
these to living a Christian life and to dying blessedly, in a loving, graceful, and comforting manner. I often attempted it and
started it, but several times I had to stop, for I recognized that
this is not a task for everyone, but only for such a person who
is well experienced in this office, who has had much practice in
dealing with the ill, who has himself tasted suffering and trials,
who has felt the sting of death, and who has the gift of comforting troubled hearts. It may well be that Satan tried to impede
this work of mine, and that he attempted to make me give it up
all together.

I, however, as the lowliest among all servants of JESUS
Christ, take pride in nothing other than in the grace of God;
and I speak obediently and humbly together with Saint Paul:
NOT I, BUT THE GRACE OF THE LORD, WHICH IS IN ME.[69] Through
such grace of my dear LORD Jesus Christ, I have at last completed it through the strength and the assistance of the Holy
Spirit; I let it come to light in God's name in which it was also
begun. I hope that this work will bring glory and honor to my
God, benefit and comfort to all my beloved, and a Christian life
and a blessed death to all guileless hearts.

The scholars I ask to treat benevolently the simple-
mindedness which I use in this little book; for this book has
been composed not for those who already have many divine
gifts and scholarly books, but for the simple-minded laypersons. I ask these unsophisticated readers to apply this work of
mine diligently and to exercise it thoroughly; I know for certain
that, thereby, they will attain salutary benefit and good avail.

How often does it happen that someone –finding himself in
strange environs– cannot find an upright minister? How often
will someone –in the midst of a military campaign or exposed
to other dangers– not be able to reach a preacher? How often
will many hearts –during times of pestilence when ministers

---

[69] 1st Corinthians 15:10.

are not present or have all died– yearn for edification, for comfort, and for instruction? Then –through this simple-minded little book– this person may award comfort to himself, or have it awarded through others who are around him and who can read –according to all measures desired by his heart– so that he will not waver but continue steadfastly on his course, and that he –through the grace of God– may have a good departure and come to a revered completion of his work.

This work of mine and this little book, my honorable and virtuous Lady, I have dedicated to you, and published under your acclaimed noble name with the comforting assurance that you, my Lady, will bear no displeasure herein which, honorable and devoted Lady, I request most subserviently. May my endeavor come as no surprise to you, my Lady; for when I had been called to the sacred preacher's office here in Sprotta eighteen years ago, as a stranger and foreigner according to the will of God, and when I faced not few contestations, especially at the beginning, your two brothers, both Lords of acclaimed memory, the noble and devoted Lord Siegfried of Nächern at Kuntzendorff and Kortnitz and the likewise noble and devoted Lord Grabes of Nächern at Buchwaldt and Dauchwitz as well as your noble, devoted, and much beloved Lord father, next to all the dear people from Sprotta –first among all children of humanity– have not only sought counsel from me and invited me, a lowly man, but have also supported me loyally. As long as God will let your brothers live, I have known them as my most generous Lords and as great friends and benefactors.

Since, after the passing of the old Lords, I remain within the blessings of their memory as well as of their much beloved children and heirs, who have bestowed on me much benevolence, whom I love and honor indeed, and whom I keep within my daily prayer; and especially you, my Lady, having been as it were orphaned a second time –not unlike having lost your beloved Lord father a few years ago– now you have lost your much beloved Lord and heart through temporal death, and you were placed into the troubled, sad state of widowhood;

therefore, I will emphasize that this little book is pledged most equitably to you, my devoted Lady, so that it will become not only a memorial of my grateful spirit toward the acclaimed dynasty of those from Nächern, but that it also become a daily handbook through which you, my Lady, may find valuable comfort.

In the name of God, I subserviently dedicate this little book to you, my devoted Lady; most subserviently requesting that you will appreciate the same, keep to it, and make good use of it; that you will deem my simple-minded endeavor most favorably and remain most gently inclined toward me. I commend you, my Lady, into God's everlasting loyal protection as well as all your much beloved children and also your Lady mother and maiden sister: to all good health and many blessings – I wish them, wholeheartedly, a blissful welfare of the body and of the soul.

At Sprotta, on Palm Sunday, the 11th of April, of the new calendar, anno 1593.

Your devoted

and at all times willingly serving

Martin Moller.

Epilogue
by Suzanne George

To GOD alone be honor. When GOD calls you, follow Him humbly and obediently. Remain steadfast when you do not understand, live blissfully as a Christian, and prepare daily for your blessed hour in death.

Martin Moller calls the *Manuale* his *simple-minded little book* which shepherds our soul's transition from fright into peace, from darkness into light, and from dying into living. Moller shows us how we can wrap our own *dear soul* in comfort throughout our daily lives *and* during our blessed departure.

Older even than the King James Bible, Martin Moller's work began nearly 500 years ago. He worked as a choir master and preacher at the age of 21 and soon applied his distinguished gift for writing. Moller's work had a great impact on readers of his time. Even Johann Sebastian Bach was inspired to write several choral cantatas based Moller's texts and hymns.

The work on *Dear Soul* began as a private and personal family project a few years ago. Before it could be made available to the public, however, it had to be completed. I hope that the presentation of this little book may serve to glorify and honor the Holy Trinity as well as you, *dear soul*. Moller's work has inspired me, led me to a better understanding and comprehension of the Bible, and graced me with a wonderful benevolence in my life's journey.

Foremost, I would like to thank the most honorable Martin Moller and all those who safeguarded and appreciated his works throughout the centuries. I would like to express everlasting gratitude to my Mom, Sandra, who harbored this work in great faith for us to carry on its magnificent message, truthfully and worthily. I also avow my loving recognition to my two sons Daniel and Derick, my daughter Manda, and my son-in-law Daniel, as well as my grandchildren for their support and involvement.

I love you all.

Daniel, my son, a special *thank you* for all the countless hours of direct involvement, the instrumental assistance in designing the book cover, and your most benevolent vision. I wish to thank friends of the family for the encouragement and support for this project, particularly for its completion. Only God's divine orchestration has made this possible.

I wish to express my gratitude to Dr. Stephen Trobisch, professional translator, who remained steadfast in his search for the right words. I thank GOD for him as he answered his calling with joy and graceful wisdom, despite the extraordinary demands of the project. Stephen spent the past several years not only translating archaic German into English, but also providing time-consuming instruction –to myself as well as my family ages 2 to 75!– in linguistics and challenges of translation, in the history of early printing technology and typesetting, and in the resulting literacy movement sweeping Europe and the entire world. I find his teaching approach and expertise quite remarkable. Thank you so much.

I would like to thank Prof. Austra Reinis for the exceptional introduction on Martin Moller and the significant history of *Ars Moriendi* – The Art of Dying. Thanks also to Dr. David Trobisch, Bible scholar, for his skilled expertise and resourcefulness, to Sheila Perryman, editor, for her brilliant reading and extraordinary research skills. Their diligent devotion to this project is beyond measure and words.

My grateful regards to Prof. Julie Johnson, classics professor, for overlooking and translating passages in Latin, to Cynthia Johnson, Jay Nicholson, and Jeff Williams graphic designers, for their instrumental contributions to the cover design, to Prof. Jonathan Crane at Emory University, Center of Ethics for his recognition of DEAR SOUL before publication implementing it into the Master of Bioethics program and the course he will be teaching, and to Quiet Waters Publications for making this book available to readers.

As we learn to walk wisely through life, it is truly with God that all things are possible. May this book offer you simple words of comfort and show you the quiet light that shines within your own *dear Soul*.

Thank you.

Suzanne George
www.dearsoulllc.com
Facebook: Dear Soul LLC

Endorsements

A Book for the Ages!

Dear Soul grows on me. It is not the kind of book you want to read all at once. Its truths are deeper than that. It is more like the Bible because everywhere you let it fall open, wisdom will greet you on any page. It is hard to do this as an e-book, but try it. Just pick a paragraph at random and read. I loved the way the translators captured the beauty and flow of Martin's language, and the spirit of living in a time so much different than our own. The words come off the page like poetry. He wrote this book for anyone who is ready to face what it means to help someone die, or to help us face the moment as Christians with courage when we must die ourselves. Pretending it is never going to happen will not stop it. So we need books like this even today to wrap ourselves in comfort and remind us that there is always hope. The advice is true and timeless, and I just keep diving back in, and going back for more. One of my favorite quotes is from one of the beautiful prayers in this book.

Safeguard me Lord Jesus. Safeguard me from a wickedly hurried death, and do not let me die in my sins.

Grant however that I commemorate my hour day and night; that I stand ready at all times in true penance, in strong faith, and in firm hope; so that I may be awake with you, and then fall asleep blissfully as you desire.

And if it pleases you to strike me with bodily weakness, here I am. I know that you are sincere and kind, and that you will not impose anything on me that is not good and blissful for me.

Grant me, however, that I will be well prepared, and that I will be a patient whose illness will serve to your honor. Amen

Reginald George, Adaptive Technology Specialist
Washington State Department Services for the Blind
Yakima, Washington

A Caring and Supportive Presence

There are not many resources that help prepare those who are facing their own deaths. *Dear Soul – A Manual for the Rightful Art of Dying* covers the spiritual side of coping with pain and with fear, and it helps prepare for the afterlife. Along with its caring and supportive presence, this could be the best book for someone facing the last stages of life, as well as for comforting their families.

Judy Warner, Haynes Ambulance of Alabama
Prattville, Alabama

Be Prepared for a Wonderful Change

Thinking of the state of affairs of our world today and the hearts and minds of many people – GOD works in wondrous ways. This morning I've been lead to know the importance of WHY this word from 500 years ago shall be revealed. There has never been a time of more need and more seeking souls – the Fields of Harvest are truly ready. This book will shake you to the core. Open your eyes to see! Open your ears to hear! Open your heart to receive! God will cleanse your heart, mind and soul. Be prepared for a wonderful change.

Sandra Cox
Missouri

So far this book leaves me speechless. I haven't made it that far but I have a hard time putting it down when I get to read.

Faith Cook
Sedalia, Missouri

A Journey of Love

Dear Soul is an impressive work of inspirational literature, and it rises far beyond place and time and Martin Moller and his "little book." Endowing rich, expressive language with the gentleness of a pastor, Martin Moller guides his readers through the difficult waters of living in cognizance of death, and of dying to the open waters of Eternal Life. This book is a journey of love undertaken by a man overcome with the love of his Savior. Writing with perseverance, even throughout the agonizing days and years of an onset of blindness, Martin Moller offers us clear and detailed guidelines for learning. He touches our souls with his kindness, challenges our hard hearts towards penance, and raises our broken spirits towards gladness and exaltation. It is my hope that this humble work, Martin Moller's remarkable *little book*, should reach all the seekers, the crushed, the broken, and even the proud to be renewed in spirit.

Priscilla Claren
Missouri

Wrapped Me in Comfort Beyond Words– Brought Me Great Peace

I am a REJOICING father, and I have grieved over the loss of my beloved son Wade who died just 5 months ago on October 26, 2013 at the age of 33. It is through GOD and my faith that I reach out to others with my story, to offer a tribute to my son, and to honor our Lord Jesus Christ.

DEAR SOUL – A Manual for the Rightful Art of Dying, along with the Bible, wrapped me in comfort beyond words. Chapters 4 and 5 brought great peace to my soul during this time. 2nd Timothy 4: 6-9 describes my son Wade in God's simple and yet profound way, and this is the only verse repeated twice in the book. DEAR SOUL is so simple to understand and easy to apply in your daily life! I hope you find words of comfort to help in your life's journey, just as my family did. I have established *Silent Warrior Ministry* in honor of my son Wade – we are a Christian Biker Fellowship. *Silent Warrior Ministry* takes GOD's word on the highway and on the roads less traveled.

GOD bless you all –

John Bryan Cook, Minister
Missouri

Find Solace in Life and Death with
Dear Soul by Martin Moller

If one were to put a highlighter to Martin Moller's, *Dear Soul: A Manual for the Rightful Art of Dying*, one would end up highlighting the entire book. While focusing on the manners of preparing for a Christian death, the content is as much about living honorably as it is about dying rightfully. Providing solace and encouragement for Christians who face affliction, illness, and suffering, Martin Moller also promotes the responsibilities which children of God must attain and by which they must live. He does not claim that the life of a child of God is easy; in fact, it is quite the opposite. Moller reveals to us how paying our penance for sins will be the most rewarding act one could ever hope to fulfill. If we seek favor with our Creator, He will release us from the bounds of worldly tribulation, and we may find comfort in eternity.

Throughout *Dear Soul*, Moller challenges not only the reader's faith, but also his or her actions in daily life. Because one does not know the time, place, nor state in which death may occur, it is vital continually to prepare for the Day of Judgment. Moller offers advice for living righteously and avoiding the temptations and perils of the world which will result in dishonorable death. Following the measures presented in this manual will ultimately enrich the lives of Christians and help them build a stronger relationship and understanding with

God. If a Christian is struggling with faith, affliction, illness, and with confronting death, then this book will help guide him or her through life's uncertainties.

Moller refers to *Dear Soul* as a *simple-minded little book*. The content of this work engages in profound notions, but they are presented so that all readers, regardless of education, may easily navigate through the text. The book is clearly arranged in a question/answer format. Moller asks a simple question, many of which the reader has likely already asked him/herself, and then he provides an answer based on Scripture. Each piece of advice on living righteously and dying rightfully is reinforced by scriptural references in each section. Readers may confidently put faith in Moller's advice, as he backs his ideas with the Word of God.

Every Christian needs to read this book. It would be an excellent curriculum tool for a group study or Sunday school class in church as it would definitely generate deep, interesting discussions. *Dear Soul* would also serve as a personal study manual as it is easy to pick up and read a section at night with the intention of reflecting on the material throughout the next day. The work has been translated carefully, and readers will find the language clear and accessible.

I would personally like to thank Suzanne George for compiling this book, and allowing me to grow spiritually through reading its contents. I urge all Christians to confront the advice offered in *Dear Soul*. Do allow Moller's writing to change and build your relationship with God as well as heal your doubts and fears regarding death.

Jay Nicholson
Missouri

Helping Us Face the Certainty of Our Death with Joy and Peace

When we reach the mid-sixties we must admit that we are in life's fourth quarter; but I believe God wants us to be able to sink a three pointer at the final buzzer! Martin Moller's book teaches us how to do exactly that. Tremendously Scriptural, extremely loving and kind, *Dear Soul* helps us face the certainty of our death with joy and peace. Praise God that he has preserved this book for over 400 years. Praise God that Suzanne George answered His call to make the *Manual* available to us.

Ron Rushley
Father of 19 children
Harrisonville, Missouri

"Bring it forth cheerfully" – Martin Moller

Dear Suzanne,
I just wanted to thank you for making it possible for English readers to read Martin Moller's writings. It was very encouraging to me, and the message of this book needs to be heard in this world in which we live. May you continue to serve the Lord with your life. And may He bless you and all who read *Dear Soul* with a greater, fuller understanding of Him. Thank you again, and thanks to all who have made this book possible. I thank God for all of you.

Sincerely,
Catherine Rushly
18-year-old daughter of Ron and Rachel Rushly

Honored to Help

I was excited to get to read two unedited pages of *Dear Soul*. It was refreshing and inspiring to see this view of an awesome story that is the Bible. I was honored to help with printing some of the artwork from the other book being translated, the Evangelium.

J.Y. Anderson
Warsaw, Missouri

These Powerful Truths Provide Peace
in the Uncertainty of Death

This Manual provides perspectives on death of both, the saved and the unsaved. Whether a believer or not, you will feel immense emotions you may never have experienced. You will awe at the truths revealed so clearly and pragmatically by Martin Moller. This book will help you understand life and death, it will make you think twice about the paths of life you choose, and it will touch deep down into expanses of the heart we all keep hidden!

Jeremy and I know not how to express our feelings on this amazing work as we already have a personal and emotional attachment to the Manual. Jeremy's father was the first to hear words read to him and one of the first to be affected by them as he lay on his death bed. Suzanne has brought Martin Moller's insight of life, of death, and of the Bible to life, and thereby she helped Jeremy's father to experience a level of peace and rest before his departure. Gary had lived a hard life, and I believe he never truly felt peace until the end. He was a believer of Christ, just not a follower. He was never one to cry, apologize, or show any emotions as to his true feelings. As death was nearing, his fears became more real and tears came more easily. This is difficult to express, but although he lay in pain and sorrow, confused and distressed, the last three weeks of his life probably were his best. Listening to the words if Martin Moller, he first struggled with allowing himself to feel hope and the peace he always needed. He eventually revealed his hidden emotions, allowing the words about life and death to grasp hold of him. His responses were no longer as harsh and bitter as when he found out about the cancer. I personally saw a transformation within him during his last days. It is difficult to fathom, and even harder to explain, how the powerful truths in this book helped him. This Manual gives basic truth of the meaning of our lives and gives peace in the uncertainty of death. It helps finding faith again, even if only for a moment.

Gary frequently listened to the following words –along with others– which I feel brought him peace:

Devotional Recitations III
The 8th Chapter

Help me, Savior, help me in fright and affliction, Have mercy on me you loyal God, I am indeed your beloved child, In spite of the world, the devil, and all sin, I trust in you, my God and Lord, When I have you, what more do I need.

Resonating with me is the following passage:

Conduct in Illness
The 4th Chapter

However, My God! I see that my illness' purpose was not for death, but for the honor of God and in praise of you, Lord Jesus Christ. For you have found compassion with me, and you have kindheartedly accepted my soul. You have tossed all my sins behind you, and you have made my life last.

This perfectly explains what happened in Dad's final days,. He came back to realizing what is most important in life, how you live it and where you will end up: in a relationship with the Lord and in Heaven beside Him!

Thank you for bringing such truths, power, and inspiration into my family. Thank you for allowing this to be a healing tool for Jeremy and his father. You generously brought this to us in time of great need. We have been blessed beyond measure with yours and Daniel's friendship! I pray that the gift you have given be returned to you manifold. We love you!

With love and warmth to you,
Jubilee and Jeremy
Missouri

A Departure *and* a Celebration

Moller's work has touched my soul primarily because of my very own near touches with death and with its incredible dignity. Being devotional, instructional, and inspirational, Moller's text provides the needed worth and respect for experiencing death as both, a departure as *and* a celebration. I pray that during the celebration of the separation of my own body and soul, someone will have the insight to read from this treasured book. Martin Moller's *Dear Soul* is a most valuable contribution to the literature for the grieving and dying as well as for those who seek words of devotion and inspiration. I have education in theology and psychology, as well as experience in private practice and in institutional psychological work.

Dr. Gary Kitto
Clinical Director of Dr. Kitto and Associates
Sedalia, Missouri

Wonderful Instruction

Dear Soul offers us wonderful instruction.

Martin Moller emphasizes our trust and faith in God, calls attention to our love for others, and puts forward the quality of our obedience needed to enter the right relationship with our Lord Jesus.

Dean L. Yoder
Warsaw, Missouri